SEW BEARably CUTE

W.J.SCOTT

Illustrations

Andrew Scott

Dr Peter T Scott

Copyright

© All rights reserved, Felix Publishing 2020

Author W. J. Scott

Illustrator Dr Peter T Scott

2020 Print edition

ISBN: 978-1-925662-10-8

2020 Digital edition

ISBN: 978-1-925662-11-5

Books 1-6 digital

ISBN: 978-1-925662-24-5   Child and Adult Aprons and Bear Applique

ISBN: 978-1-925662-25-2   Simple Bears

ISBN: 978-1-925662-28-3   Shaped Bears

ISBN: 978-1-925662-29-0   Simple Dolls and Bears

ISBN: 978-1-925662-30-6   Bear Blankie

ISBN: 978-1-925662-31-3   Cubby House

Other books in this series Make Life Simpler by W. J. Scott:

The Perfect Assignment

ISBN: 978-0-9945755-7-9

Debt Free the Morals of Money Management

ISBN: 978-0-9945755-1-7

Libre de Deuda, de la moral de la administración del dinero

ISBN: 978-0-9945755-1-7

Swift, Simple, Sweet!

ISBN: 978-0-9945755-3-1

Registration: Thorpe-Bowker, Level 1 607 St Kilda Rd Melbourne, Victoria 3000 Australia
bowkerlink@thorpe.com.au

No part of this publication may be reproduced, stored in a retrieval system, or transmitted in any form or by any means, electronic, mechanical, photocopying, recording or otherwise, without the prior written permission of the author or a license permitting restricted copying for educational institutions.

SEW BEARABLY CUTE
W. J. SCOTT

Make children's aprons

Sew teddies on any fabric or clothing

Make cute little mascot teddies

Make larger cuddly teddies as gifts

Sew comforter bear blankie

Sew an indoor cubby house

No previous sewing skills required!

Hand or machine stitched

Made in less than a day

All can be made from leftovers or remnants, in fact this is the best choice including memories and saving waste.

Contents:

Book 1:

Choosing Fabric

How to Thread a Needle

Running Stitch, Back Stitch, Ladder Stitch and Overcasting Stitch

Apron with Applique, Adult and Child

Applique Bear

Book 2:

Lavender Bag

Lavender Bear-Felt

Lavender Bear- Cotton

Basic Bear Stuffed

Dressing Up Basic Bear

Bear in Various Sizes

Book 3:

Shaped Grizzly/Polar Bear

Styling Your Unique Bear, Wedding/Bikie /Floral/Christmas

Book 4:

Simple Dolls

Simple Rabbits

Simple Bears

Simple Mouse

Book 5:

Bear Blankie (Baby Cuddle Blanket Square)

Book 6:

Cubby House (Play House /Wendy House)

Book 1

These booklets are for experienced as well as absolute beginners to sewing. Book 6 needs confidence in using a sewing machine. If you experience any difficulty in understanding these directions, or want to send a photo of your wonderful creations, send an email to info.felixpublishing@gmail.com we will respond with any help or feedback.

Choosing Fabric

If this is your first project never use expensive fabric to learn, you are so worried about making a mess you will never finish it. Re purposing and recycling are great ways of saving your sanity and the planet.

The fabric is chosen using 3 criteria:

1. How or where is the item to be used, and by whom.
2. What will look the best.
3. What you have as leftovers, cheaply available, are there any allergies of the user etc.

1. A. If the item is the first project, a child's apron with or without matching adult version, these are the considerations.

    *If used for painting it needs to be thick and washable, preferably cheap and easily replaced when it no longer folds away as it is too encrusted with (no longer washable) paint. Offcuts of gabardine, curtaining, and washable cotton with a little polyester so that it does not look too horrible just off the line. Adult aprons need not be as durable allowing lovely printed cottons, calico, gingham and gabardine. At Grandma's house painting aprons are in gabardine with the children's names on them, at playgroups they are sheet plastic.

*Old sheets double thickness work well and look rather cute with colourful appliques and or painted designs. Torn towels can be recycled well if you avoid the rips when cutting out the apron.

1B. if you are making the bear to applique avoid thick pile like fur fabrics, use velvet, velour, polar fleece, track suiting inside out or terry towelling for texture. Any colour any fabrics work for applique except gauzy types for the basic outline, these are fine for detail though. Cottons in any pattern or thickness work very well here.

1C. if you are making a mascot bear for an adult, any fabric will do as long as it is not fine and gauzy. For fine details in shaping and a fine smooth finish, fabrics that have a little stretch, will give you the best result.

1D. if you are making a teddy or blanket with a head (blankie), specifically for children to use, soft polar fleece, fine fake fur fabric, soft old blanket, cotton knits, or smooth cotton is ideal. Make sure that it is machine washable and is not affected by nappy soakers, similarly use hollow fibre Dacron for stuffing, sanitised old pillow stuffing or pantyhose if you still wear them in cold weather. It is so upsetting when the toy does not survive the first wash.

NEVER USE REMOVABLE EYES, BUTTONS, OR SHARP OBJECTS ON TOYS FOR CHILDREN UNDER FIVE YEARS OLD. They *will* chew it, they could choke, or swallow it.

2. When choosing what will look the best

*Think of how durable the fabric is. Will it take what a child hands out? Will it tear in the struggle to remove it by the independent hands of a 3 year old?

> Aprons and appliques for young children think gabardine, old sheets, old blankets, terry towelling, backed curtaining.
>
> For toys, old blankets, terry towelling, panne velvet, lawn, satin, faux fur (only for more experienced), cottons, track suiting and corduroy.
>
> For older children washable and durable are the only considerations.
>
> For adult aprons, backed curtaining for heavy use, gabardine for standard, and pretty fabrics for decoration only.
>
> Adult mascot bears whatever you like, it is easier to use something with a bit of stretch to give a nice finish on curved seams.

*will it wash, will it fade. Will it shrink when washed to remove paint, and glue and glitter?

*what colours does the recipient prefer? Never use brown for someone who loves pink and purple, nor use pink for a lover of earthy tones. Colour preferences tend to go in groups,

> PINKS choose pink, purple, blue, red, orange and rainbow shades.
>
> GREEN choose green, blue, yellow, rust, brown.

BLUE choose blue, green, purple, yellow, aqua.

BROWN choose brown, yellow, orange, khaki, olive.

*Is the recipient a touchy feely person or a more formal personality who prefers standard predictable styles?

Traditional taste, smooth cottons and gabardine

Feely, velvet, satin, terry towel, organza, lace

Very feminine, satin, lace, velvet, organza, floral

Outdoors, gabardine, hessian, rugged cottons

Bohemian, flouncy fabrics with colour and movement

*does the recipient follow fashion, if so check what styles and fabrics are trending.

3. These patterns are designed to use up scraps and leftovers to convert them into something to love. If you bought trousers that were too long and you have the off cuts great, a little bear to match, and trimmings from a wedding dress to make a little bear as a keepsake. Red fabric on sale after Christmas, perfect, my son's bear is red thick pile left over from a bomber jacket I made when he was three. The jacket was given to charity when he grew out of it but the bear remains. Bears can be made from sentimental fabrics as well as fabrics given by friends, bought from charity stores, or on clearance in remnant bins. Only buy fabric specifically when you have already confidently made the pattern. It is also fun to make a shirt and make a bear to match out of leftovers.

How to Thread a Needle

Cut thread at an angle with **sharp** scissors. If you use blunt scissors or break the yarn there will be a long furry end making threading difficult.

Hold the eye of the needle vertically between thumb and first finger of left hand (right if left handed) with the eye facing your right hand. Hold the trimmed thread in your right hand 1 cm (1/2 inch) from the end.

Push the thread between the fingers of your left hand. That is through the eye of the needle. This works even if you need glasses to see and cannot see the hole.

Pull the thread through to no longer than the distance between your finger and elbow.

The length is important for two reasons:

> Long threads tangle and knot.

> Long threads mean that you could accidently stab someone nearby with the needle as you pull it through, really not good for relationships.

Tie the two ends together and cut the thread.

If you only need a single thickness thread, do not tie the knot through both threads just knot the longer end.

When you are more adept at sewing you will not knot the thread as frequently but do two running stitches on the same spot.

Running Stitch, Back Stitch, Ladder Stitch and Overcasting Stitch

Running Stitch

Thread the needle, double the thread over, tie a knot in the end or perfectly match the ends and stitch twice over the same spot.

Insert the needle at the end of the stitch line on the front of the seam.

Pull through to the back of the fabric, making sure the fabric edges are perfectly matched.

From the back insert the needle 3 threads further along the stitch line and pull through to the front. Keep the thread taut but do not pucker the fabric.

Repeat.

Keep the stitches an equal distance from each other and the edge.

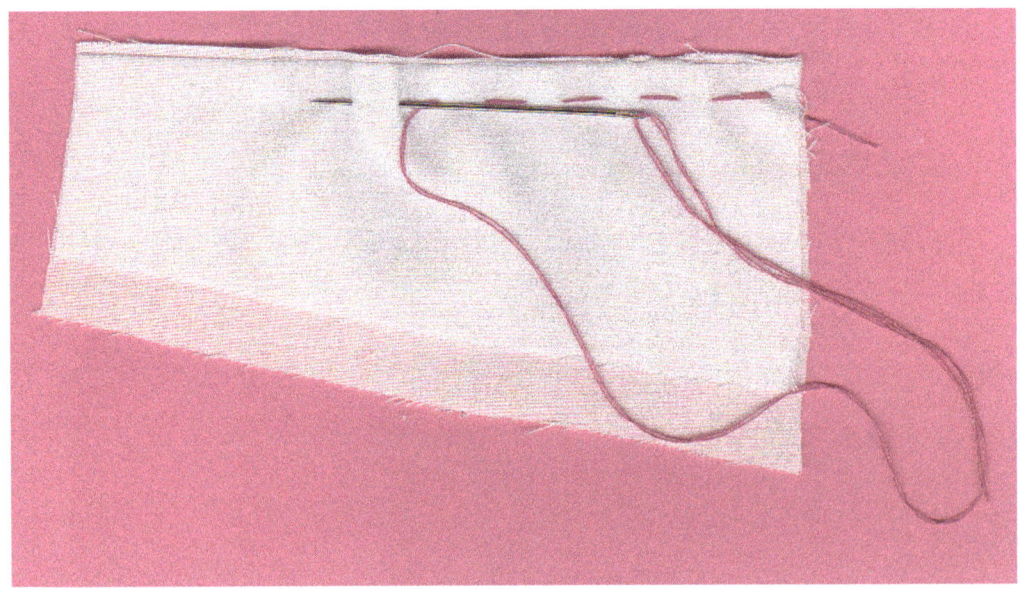

Running stitch

Back Stitch

Back stitch is a stronger stitch, ideal for sewing the main seams in the teddies.

Back stitch as the name suggests is sewn with the needle always starting from behind where the thread emerges, not ahead, but the needle still points in the direction sewn.

Start with a double stitch to secure the thread.

Take the needle from front to back of fabric.

Take the needle forward one stitch and push through to front.

Take the needle from front to back of fabric.

Take the needle forward one stitch and push through to front.

This will give a continuous row of stitches on the front, like machine stitches and a crossover row of stitches on the back.

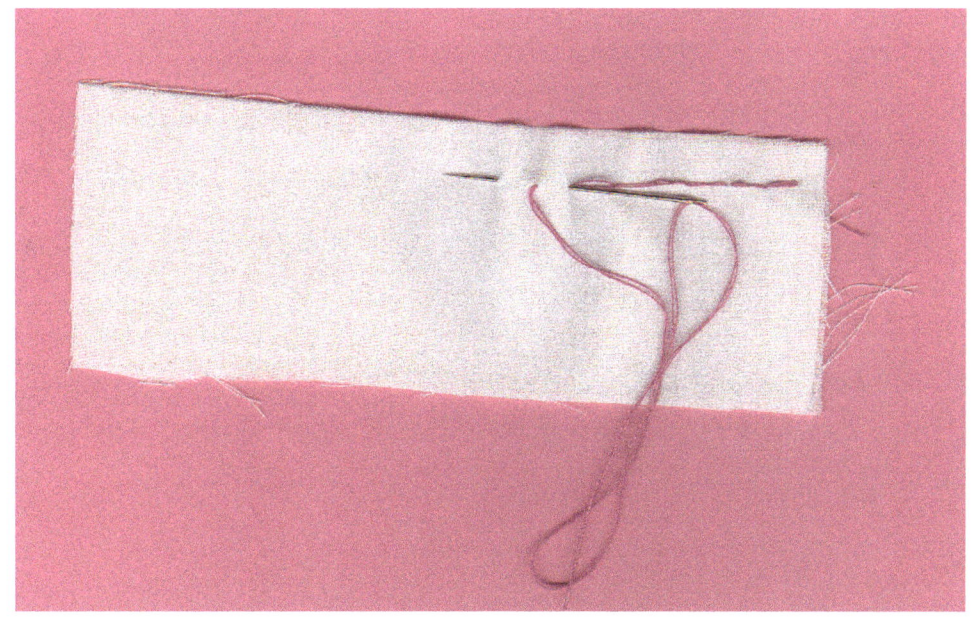

Front of back stitch

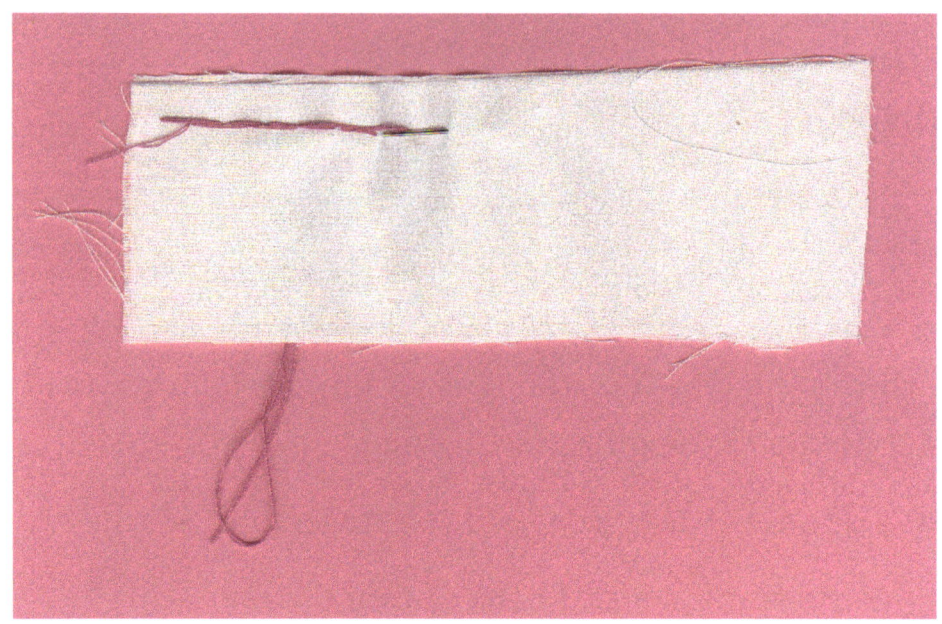

Back of back stitch

Ladder Stitch

Ladder stitch is used to neatly close seams, invisibly after stuffing.

It is the simplest of all stitches after running stitch.

After threading the needle and putting a knot in the end insert the needle in the fold of the seam on one side, go up one stitch, then out. Do the same on the other side and repeat. Pull firmly but do not pucker.

The stitches should be horizontal like steps on a ladder to give a smooth unpuckered seam on the belly of the bear. This is certainly not where you want to draw attention to the stitching. Matching thread is very important here.

In the photo I have used black thread on light green to make the stitches visible, it is also highly magnified.

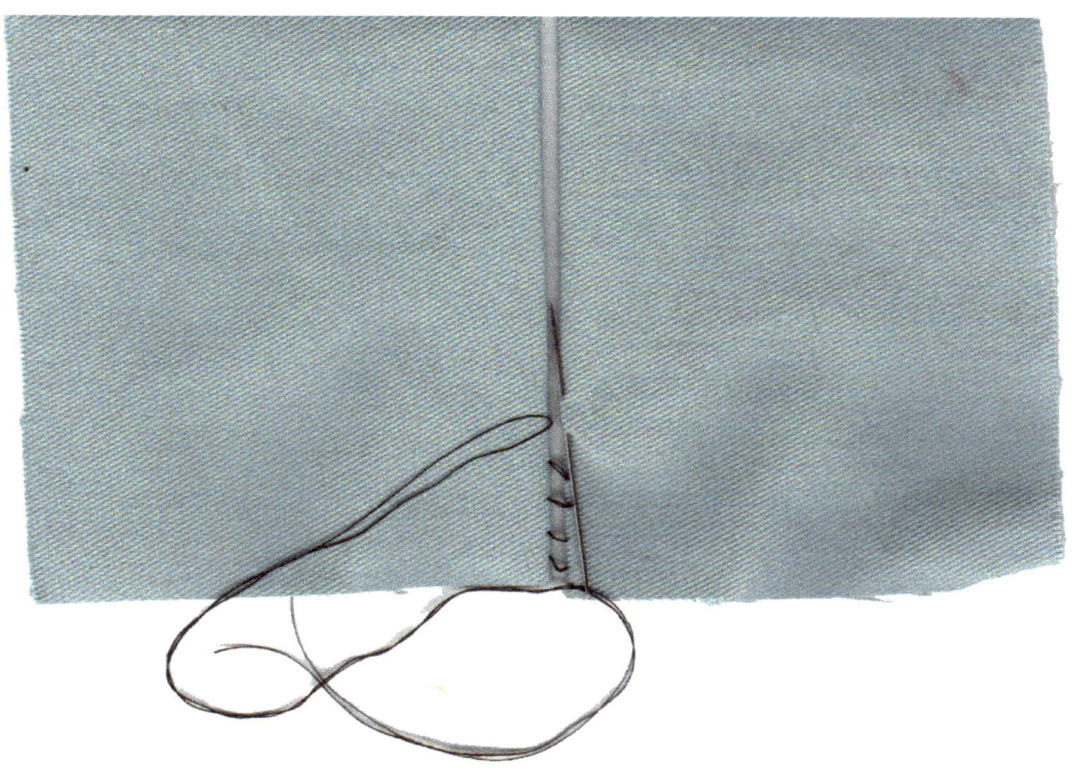

Ladder stich open for detail

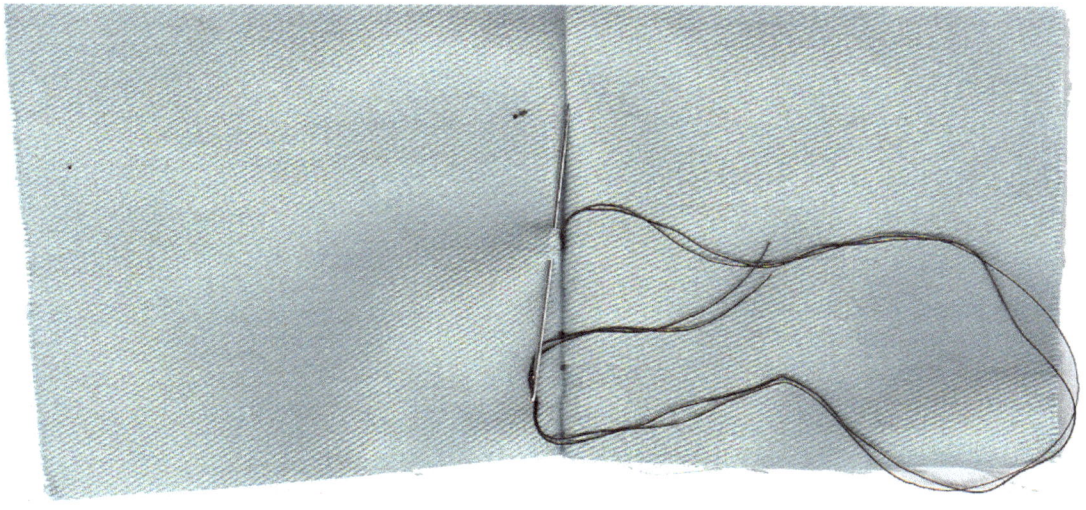

Ladder stitch closed to show finish

Overcasting Stitch

This is the stitch that most people given a threaded needle will chose to do if they have no sewing experience. It is a natural easy movement.

You can use it to hand applique onto a garment if not using a sewing machine. Do not over use this stitch. Never use this to make a teddy, it will ruin the effect.

Thread the needle put a knot in the end.

Insert needle the width of the oversew from the back to the front. Now repeat this advancing an even spacing, .3 to .4 cm is ideal.

Use small close stitches on fine fabrics and larger more widely spaced stitches on thick fabric.

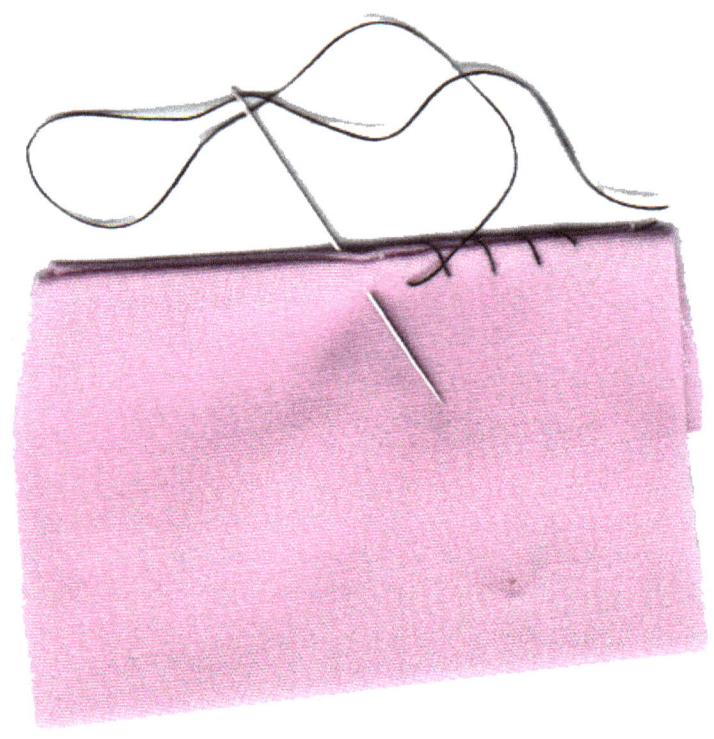

Oversewing a seam

Apron with Applique, Adult and Child

Child and adult aprons

Child apron materials:

Print or copy this pattern.

Cut it out and stick it to newspaper to extend the length by 28 cm as shown on the pattern.

60cm (24") X 40cm (15") fabric

Tape or extra matching fabric for ties. 2x 50 cm for waist ties plus one 45cm strip for neck strap.

Machine with sewing thread, or hand sew if desired.

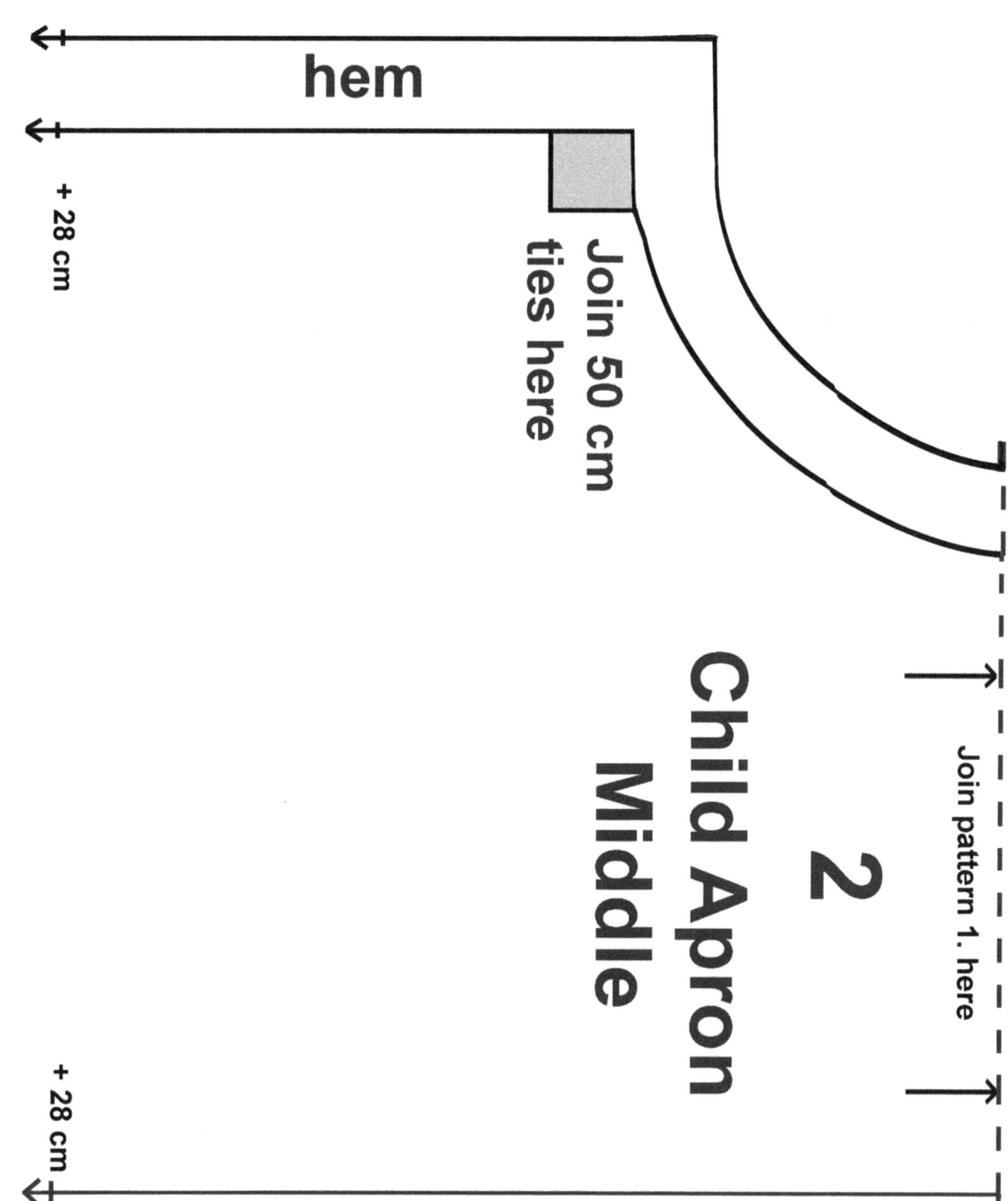

This is a full sized pattern, print it, attach to newspaper, and measure the added length. Alternatively you can trace the pattern onto greaseproof or tissue paper for a more flexible pattern.

The best way to make the pattern is use a roll of greaseproof paper, trace the top half of the pattern, mark end of pattern. Then continue on the same paper lining up the ends, mark out the middle. Mark the ends again and continue with the bottom of the pattern.

Transfer the markings, write on it what it is, and cut it roughly beyond the edges. This will give you a permanent pattern that is easy to reuse.

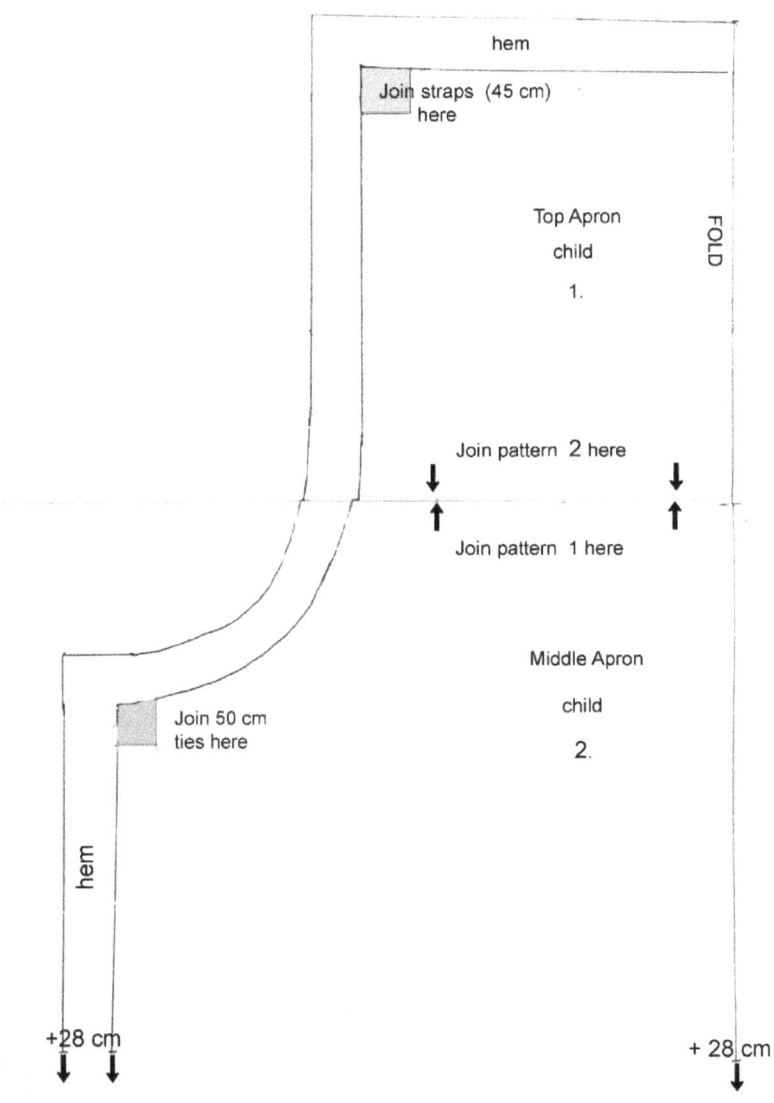

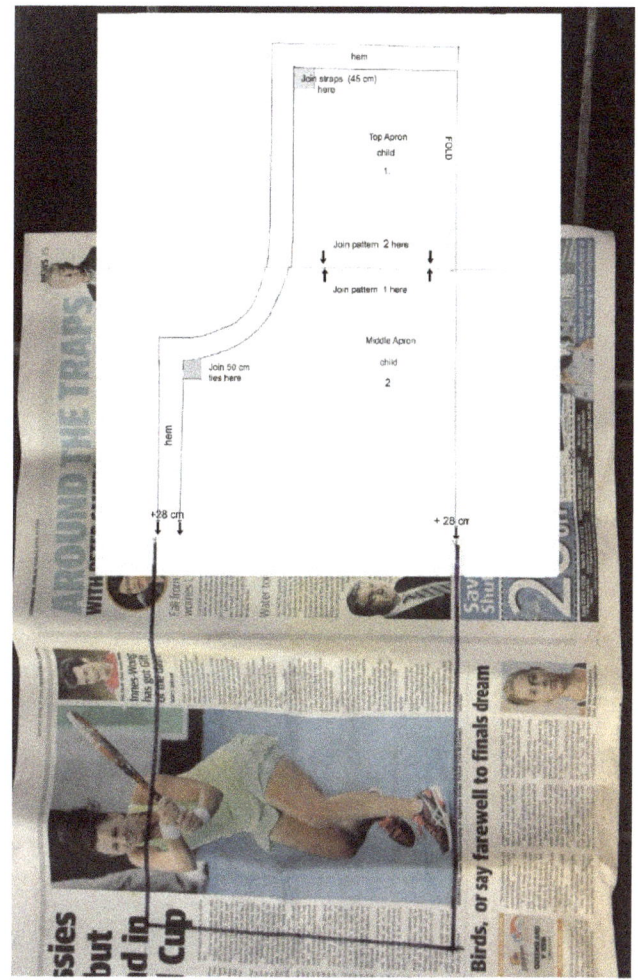

Apron pattern ready to cut out

Cutting out the pattern:

Fold the fabric long ways with a nice neat fold. Crumpled edges will give a messy edge and be inaccurate.

Pin around the edges of the pattern, making sure the edge of the pattern marked fold is indeed on the fold. Putting in the pins at right angles to the cutting line will make it easier to cut neatly. Make sure the pins do not go beyond the edge of the pattern.

Now, using large dressmaker's scissors cut smoothly in long strokes through both layers of fabric together, this will give the neatest finish, little snipping strokes leave a jagged edge that is very hard to tidy.

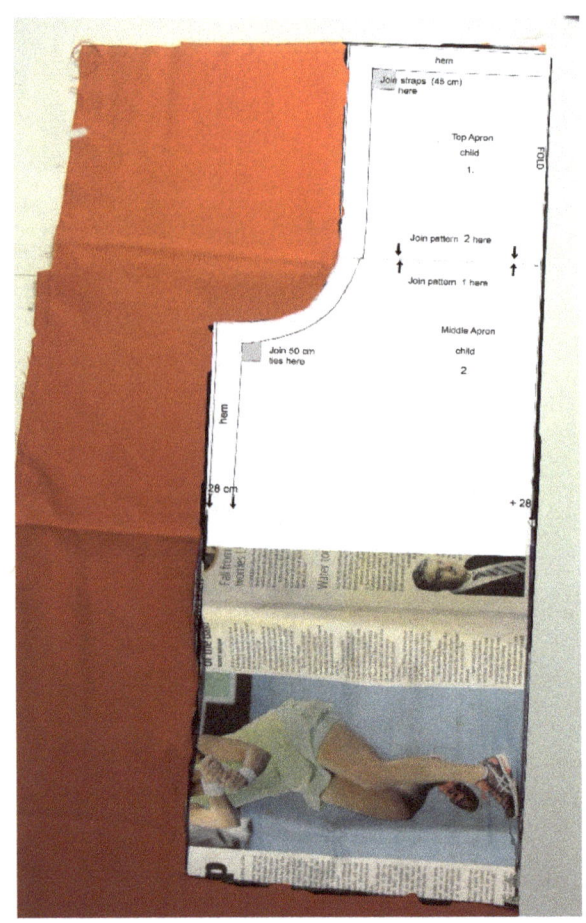

Note the fabric is on the fold just here   ^

If you are not using tape for the ties cut the straps from that lovely fabric on the side. The neck ties can be two separate ties that are tied in a bow at the back or a pre measured tie that attaches to both sides of the top at the front. This is preferred for young children when you can get them to hold still for measuring, also if making for yourself. Any gifts always do the two ties guaranteeing perfect fit. Cut random shapes of the same fabric or contrast for pockets if you wish. When I sold the children's aprons in a gift shop, I could not keep up supply of little aprons with a small pocket that I put either a tiny teddy or small packet of six colouring pencils.

Check that you have all the pieces, the whole apron, neck ties and waist straps. Match the thread as closely as possible to the fabric.

Unless you are a brilliant tailor and highly experienced this is a cardinal rule to make the stitches disappear. To make a pocket, pin the apron on yourself or child, find the comfortable position for resting hand, mark the bottom with a pin on the apron, not on the child no matter how irascible they are. Now trace round the spread hand on paper, allow seams then draw your shape. Voila, the perfect position and size.

Sewing the apron:

If you have access to an overlocker and can use it safely, overlock right around the outside edges of the main apron.

If you do not have an overlocker or sufficient experience to use it safely turn a narrow edge under before folding the rest of the hem.

Fold under and stitch round the outside using matching thread with 1.5cm (5/8") hem all round. Use a straight machine stitch, a running stitch or a simple overcast stitch (needle into edge of hem and main fabric, move forward .3cm or ¼" and repeat).

If using matching fabric for straps, neaten the edges with an overlocker or turn a narrow hem on each side before attaching to the apron.

Attach 45cm strap to top for neck strap. Fold over ends to stop fraying.

Join 50cm (1/2 yd.) straps to the sides. Put on applique if desired.

Adult apron in Christmas print

Adult Apron

Use child apron but add 4cm to width of pattern at the fold line, and add 10 cm to pattern between piece 1 and 2. Lengthen it to your choice.

Use longer ties, 60cm for neck and 1 metre ties at waist.

Make it on newspaper or butcher paper to keep as a permanent pattern.

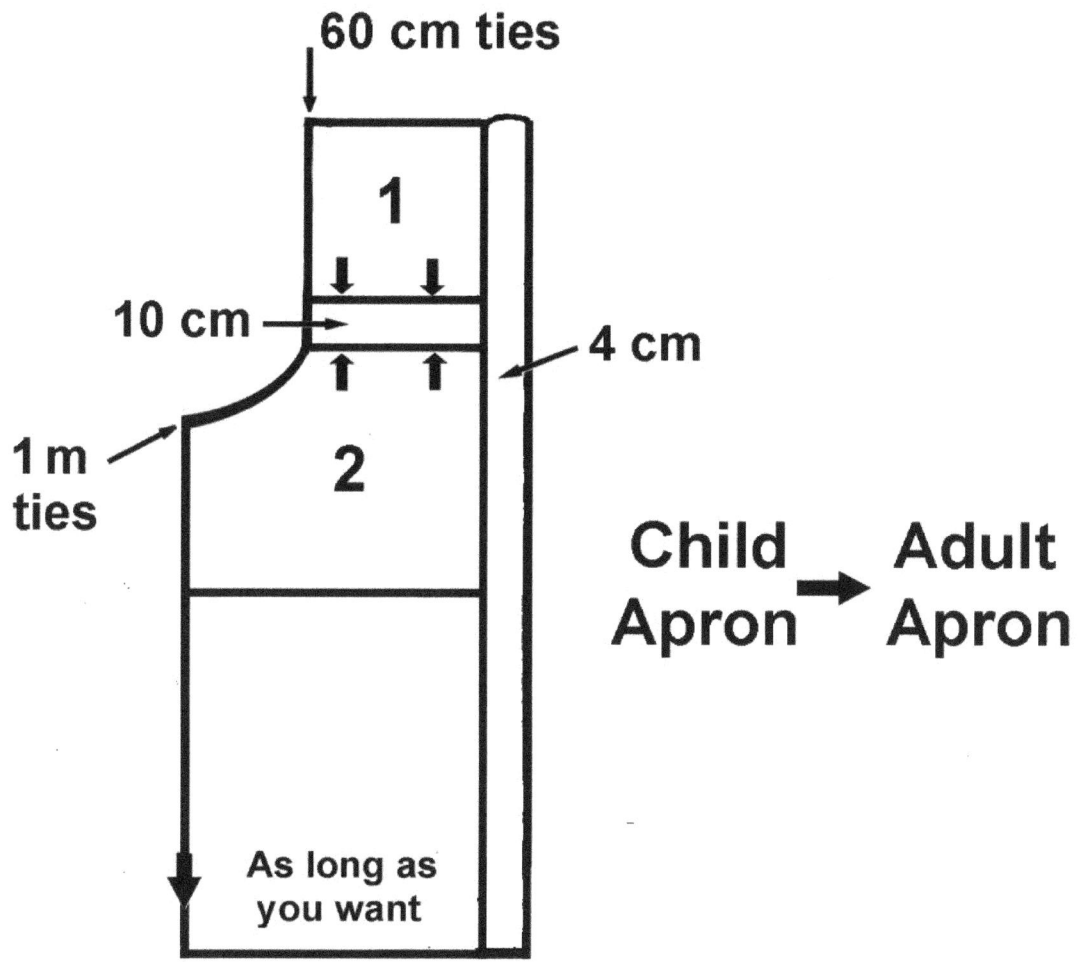

Applique Bear

Materials:

8cm of Vliesofix or Heat and Bond

Scrap of fabric 8cm square

Fabric or clothing to decorate (apron, shirt, quilt square)

Fabric paint for features or embroidery thread.

Matching fabric for outline or thread for stitching.

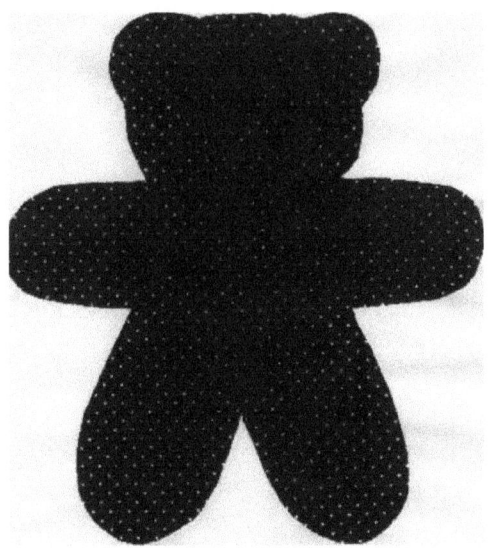

Photocopy, trace or print this pattern, *but NEVER use it to make items for sale or give it to others to use that is a copyright breach.*

If using the print version of this book trace pattern straight onto the back (the smooth side) of Vliesofix or Heat n Bond. If using the digital version printout the page nominating A4 as the size, trace the pattern from your printout.

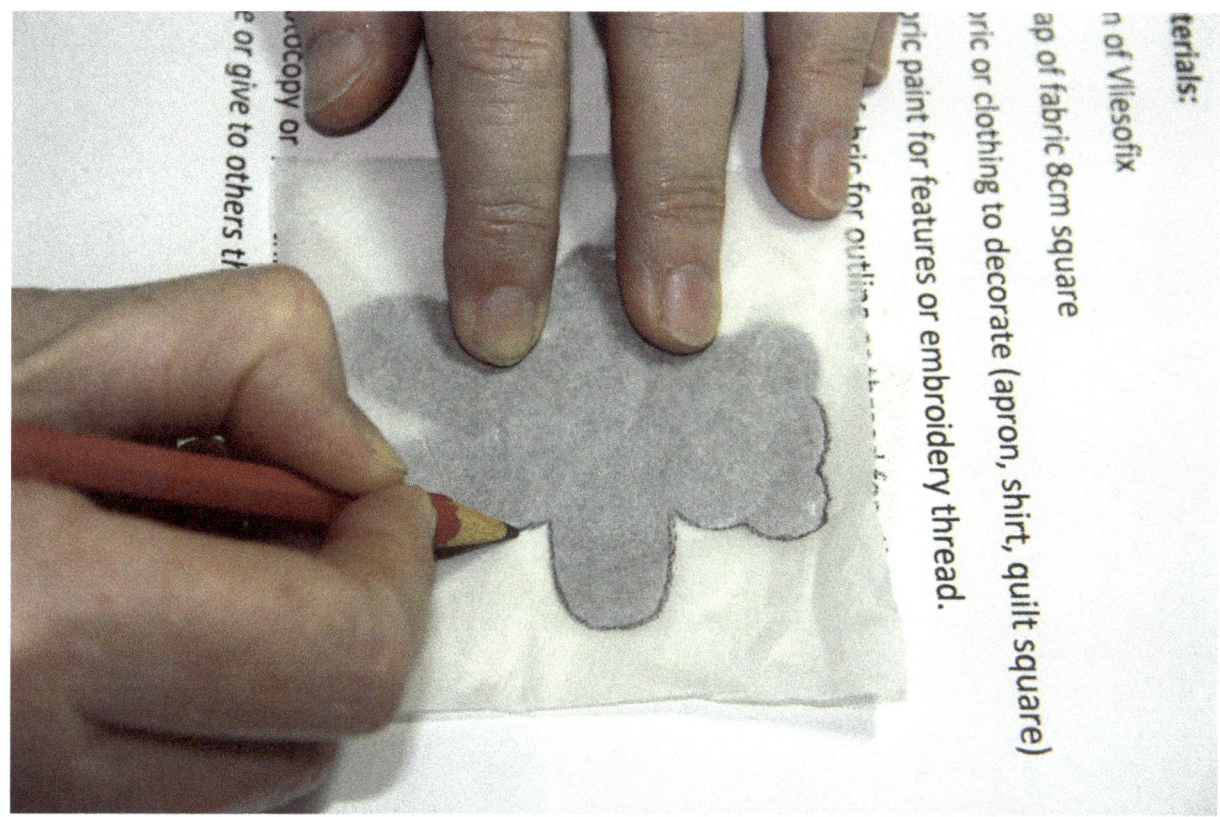

Cut roughly around the Vliesofix just bigger than the outline.

Put the rough side of the Vliesofix on the WRONG SIDE of the bear fabric.

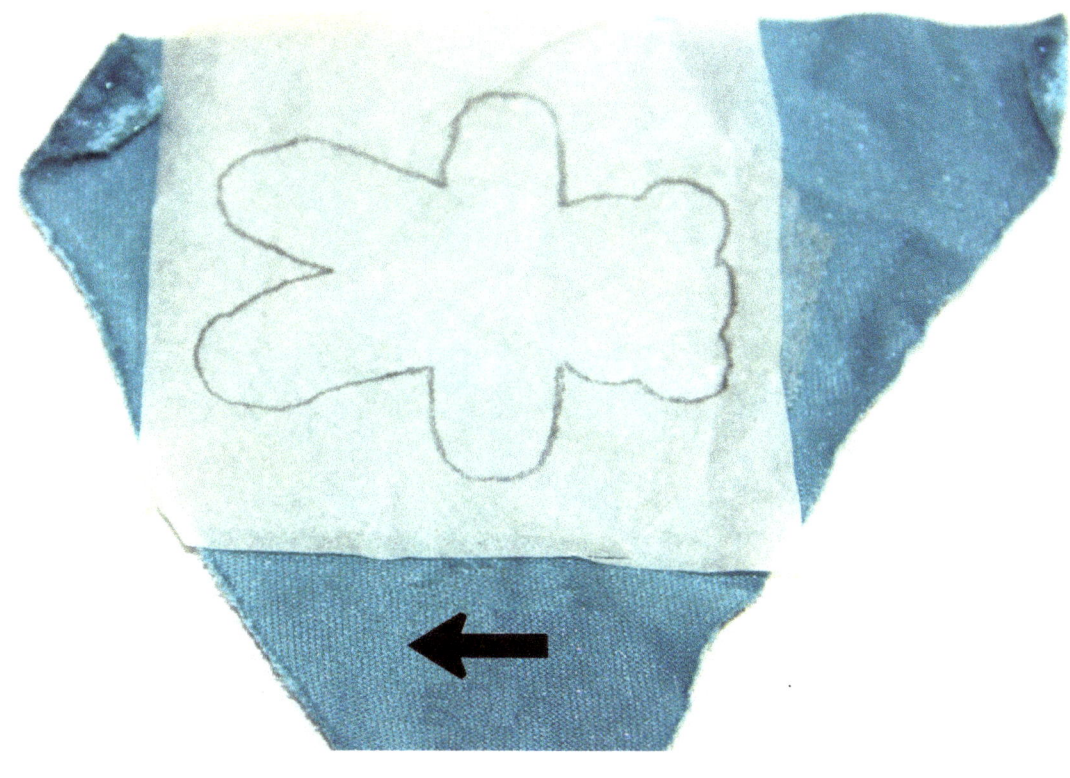

Press using an iron medium heat but NO STEAM. Those are the only things that usually go wrong here.

Let the fabric cool for 5 minutes then check that it has adhered properly.

Cut exactly along the outline of the bear.

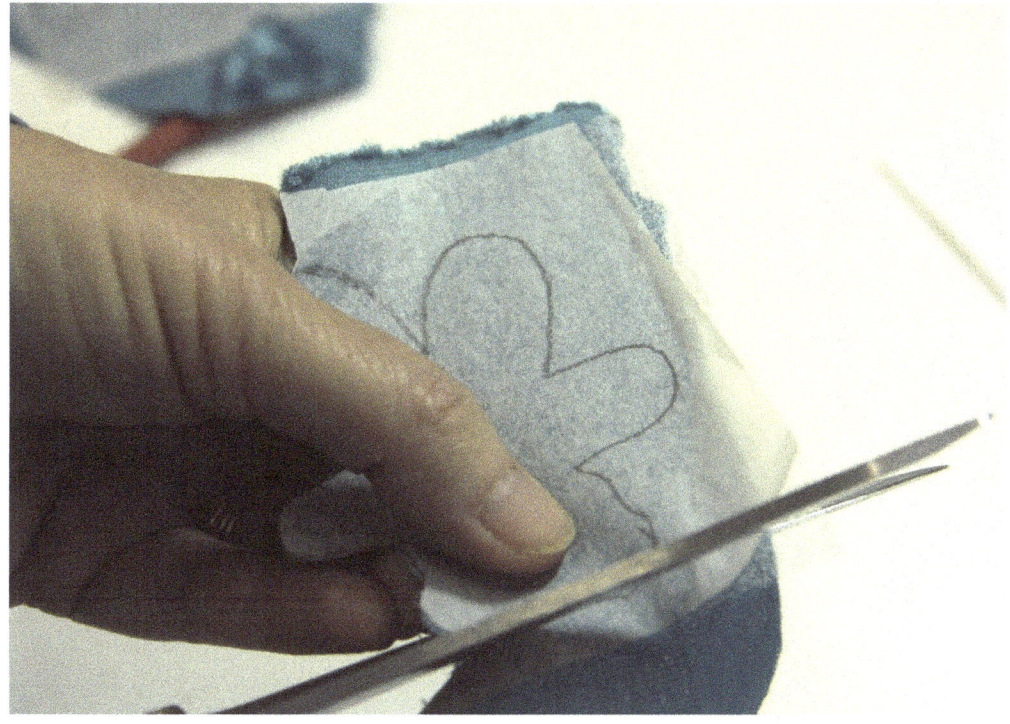

Peel the paper off the back of the bear.

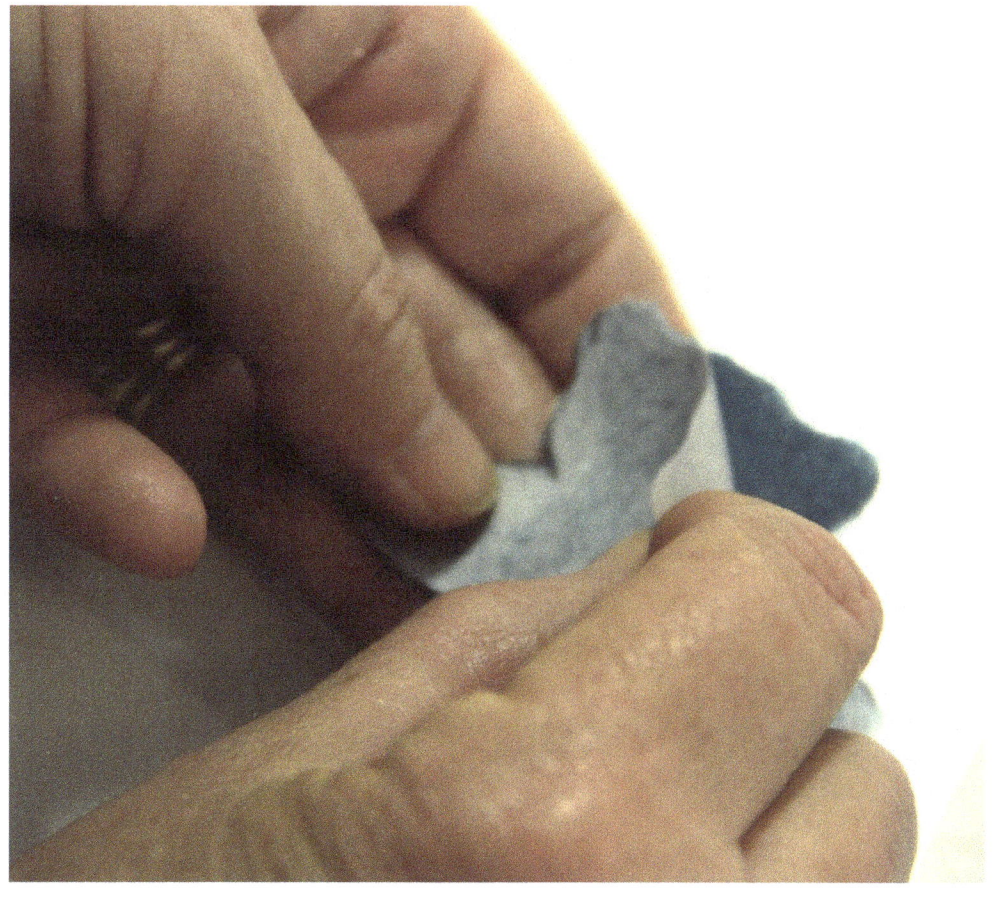

Carefully line it up where you want the applique.

If you are using a ribbon tuck the ends in under the bear before ironing, this will actually glue the ends under, neat trick.

If you are using synthetic fabric for bear, cover it with a cloth before pressing or you will scorch it.

Make sure the bear is face up on the right side of the garment, press with **warm dry iron**. Let it cool.

1. Stitched version:

Either stitch by machine or hand with zigzag or blanket or satin stitch round the outside of the bear and across the base of his ears.

Then using embroidery thread sew little knots for eyes and a rounded w for mouth, then a black triangle for a nose.

Sew on a bow if you wish round his neck.

2. Non stitched version:

Using fabric paints choose either contrast or perfect match for outline, black for features. This is ideal for children's aprons but is not durable enough for heavy use.

Put 2 thicknesses of newspaper under the garment. Do not leave this step out or the paint will ruin everything nearby.

Using a matching or contrasting colour fabric paint over the edges of the bear, and across the base of the ears.

Using black, put blobs of paint for eyes, a triangle of black for nose, extend this with a rounded w for mouth. Put it aside to dry for 24 hours. Do not let anything touch it or get it wet during this time. After 24 hours remove the newspaper. It is ready for use.

Book 2:

Lavender Bag

Lavender bags are a great way to freshen clothes and keep moths and insects away from your valuable clothes without harsh smelly chemicals, and are environmentally responsible. When they lose their fragrance a few drops of lavender oil and it is back to perfect again. It is said that lavender oil is a relaxant that aids sleep so one of these near the pillow should improve sleep, if nothing else, it will remove mustiness.

Materials:

Small scrap of thin summer weight fabric, cotton, net, lace gauze

Dried lavender or potpourri.

Method:

Cut a rectangle of fabric no larger than 17 cm by 14cm.

Fold through the middle of the long side.

Stitch across the base and long side.

Turn inside out, use a ruler or pencil to gently push out the corners to square.

¾ fill with dried lavender blossoms or potpourri.

Fold the top down inside so that no raw edges are visible, hand or machine sew closed.

Stitching sides on lavender bag.

Lavender bag filled and stitched closed

That last lavender bag was too easy, after you have made 40 or more for well received presents you will be bored. Lavender Bear is a way to do the same thing in a fun shape.

Lavender Bear-felt

Bear pattern

Materials:

Felt offcut 14cmx16cm

Tiny offcut net, organza or lace 14cmx16cm

Lavender flowers or potpourri

Black fabric paint or embroidery thread, wobbly eyes if wanted

Scrap of ribbon for bow.

Instructions:

Digital readers print out the pattern nominate A4. Cut around the outline.

Print book readers use greaseproof paper and trace the pattern from the previous page, or scan it and cut it out (the scan, not the book, but you knew that).

Lay net over felt, pin pattern on top. Have right sides out. Make sure that you can see the edges of both fabrics, it saves the upset of finding that one layer is missing an arm as the fabric underneath was not wide enough or folded under.

Cut around both layers of fabric at the same time.

Cut exactly on the lines.

Remove the pattern, repin the pieces together.

Lavender bear cut out

To remove smear such as near the mouth rub with methylated spirits before stuffing. It will disappear like magic. Make sure that you leave fabric paint undisturbed for 24 hours or you too will have smears.

The pictured bear is organza spot and cotton sheeting, this allows maximum ventilation and effectiveness for the lavender. Using felt underneath makes it easier to sew and it holds its shape better. For a first effort use felt if you have it. Note, *if* you have it. Do not buy fabrics for any of your first efforts ask family and friends who sew or use old clothes that were heading to duty as dusters. Without the worry of wasting fabric and making a mess you are most likely to be successful.

First sew across the base of ears this shapes the bear and stops the filling from distorting the bear. Then sew the outline.

Lavender bear, lace front

Either sew by hand or machine .3cm from edges all the way around leaving a 2cm gap along the straight edge of the leg for stuffing.

Hand sewing use running, backstitch or blanket stitch.

Machine sewing use straight, zigzag or satin stitch.

Loosely fill with lavender, shaking it into legs arms and head as well as belly. Make a paper funnel to make the pouring easier. Fill the head first, then arms then the leg that is sewn and belly, leaving the open leg to last. If you change the order you will be unable to fill the arms, legs and head properly.

Now stitch the last 2 cm of the outside seam.

To decorate: paint little black dots for eyes, a little dot for a nose join to a tiny w for mouth, and tie ribbon to a bow at neck.

Well done. Mass produce these as presents for family and friends to keep moths at bay.

Lavender bear complete

Lavender Bear - cotton

Materials:

2 pieces of pretty fabric 14cm x 16cm

Dried lavender

Small ribbon for neck bow

Fabric paint or embroidery thread for features

Instructions:

Lay both pieces of fabric, wrong sides together, pin pattern on top. Cut exactly on the lines.

Remove the pattern, repin the pieces together.

Either sew by hand or machine .3cm from edges all the way around leaving a 2cm gap for stuffing.

Hand sewing use running, backstitch or blanket stitch.

Machine sewing use straight, zigzag or satin stitch.

Clip all of the curves up to but not through the stitching, if you leave out this step it will wrinkle at all the curves and could possibly tear during stuffing.

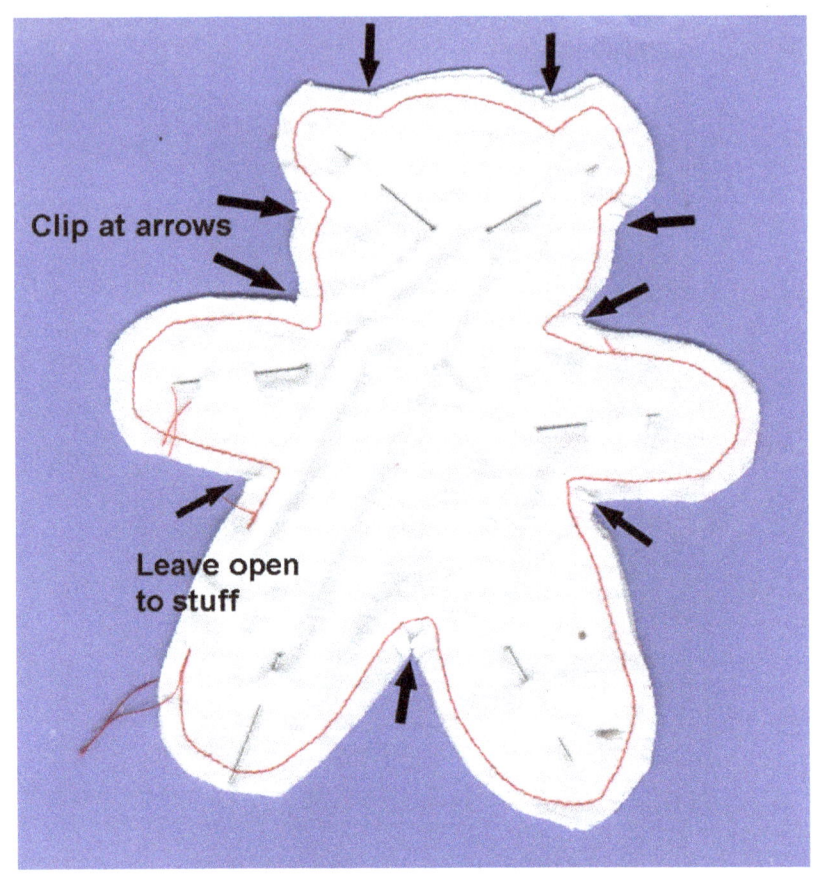

Now to turn the bear right side out.

Step 1 use finger to push the ears inside the head.

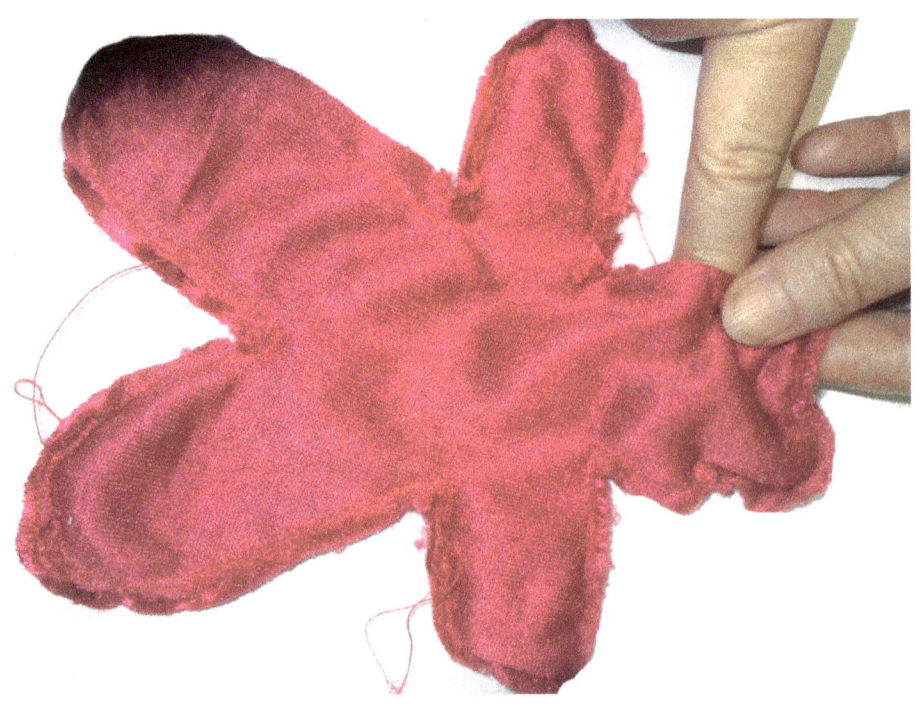

Step 2 use finger to push the head inside belly.

Step 3 use finger to push the arms inside the belly

Step 4 use finger to push the stitched leg out through the open leg.

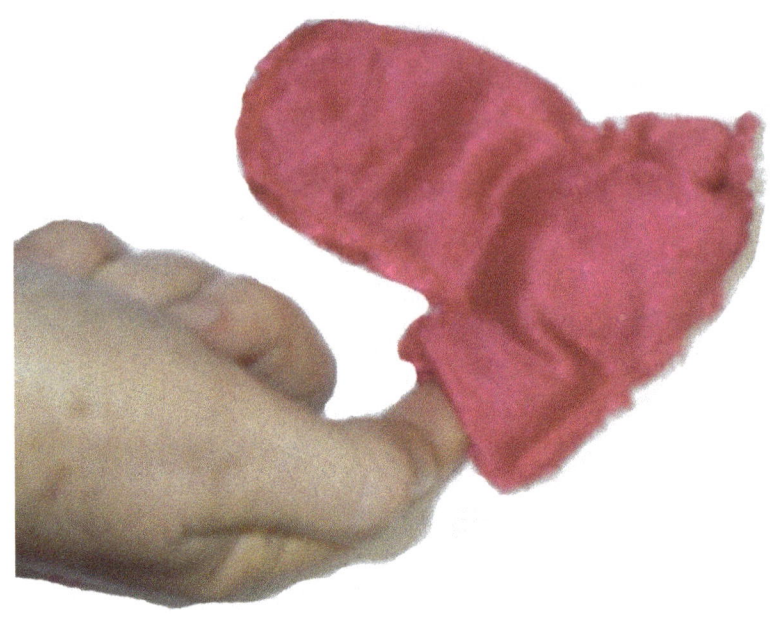

Step 5 use finger to push the rest out behind the leg, turn the open leg right side out.

Simple, wasn't it. Get the order wrong and a major tangle will ensue.

Roll the seams between thumb and index finger to make the seams come right to the edge.

Now sew across base of the ears as indicated.

Loosely fill with lavender, shaking it into legs arms and head as well as belly. Make a paper funnel to make the pouring easier. Fill the head first, then the leg, then arms and belly, do the opened leg last. If you change the order you will be unable to fill the arms, legs and head properly.

Now stitch the last 2 cm of the outside seam. Do this by hand using ladder stitch.

To decorate: paint little black dots for eyes, a little dot for a nose join to a tiny w for mouth, and tie ribbon to a bow at neck. You can glue wobbly eyes on if it is not to be near a child under 5.

Basic teddy done in panne velvet

Basic Bear Stuffed

Bear pattern

Materials:

2 pieces of pretty fabric 14cm x 16cm

Hollow fill Dacron, polyester fibre, sanitised pillow stuffing, old pantyhose

Small ribbon for neck bow

Fabric paint or embroidery thread for features.

Instructions:

If using fur fabric, velvet, satin, panne velvet etc. read instructions at the end first.

Lay both pieces of fabric, **wrong** sides together, pin pattern on top. Cut exactly on the lines.

Remove the pattern, repin the pieces together.

Either sew by hand or machine .3cm from edges all the way around leaving a 2cm gap for stuffing.

Hand sewing use running, backstitch or blanket stitch.

Machine sewing use straight, zigzag or satin stitch.

Clip all of the curves up to but not through the stitching, if you leave out this step it will wrinkle at all the curves and could possibly tear during stuffing. See picture earlier in this chapter.

Now to turn the bear right side out. See pictures in previous section.

Step 1 use finger to push the ears inside the head.

Step 2 use finger to push the head inside belly.

Step 3 use finger to push the arms inside the belly

Step 4 use finger to push the stitched leg out through the open leg.

Step 5 use finger to push the rest out behind the leg, turn the open leg right side out.

Stitch across the base of ears, do a curved seam to round the bear's face.

Fill with Dacron or alternative, gently pressing it into legs arms and head as well as belly. Press the outside until you are certain that it is neither too tightly nor too loosely stuffed. Fill the head first, then the leg, then arms and belly, do the opened leg last. If you change the order you will be unable to fill the arms, legs and head properly.

Now stitch the last 2 cm of the outside seam. Do this by hand using ladder stitch.

To decorate: paint little black dots for eyes, a little dot for a nose join to a tiny w for mouth, and tie ribbon to a bow at neck. You can glue wobbly eyes on if it is not to be near a child under 5.

This bear is very basic, he or she is cuddly and great fun, you can use basically any fabric except very long pile fur for the small size. Personalising the bear is the greatest fun.

When you gain confidence to use stretch or fur pile fabrics there are a few simple things to get a great finish.

Stretch Fabrics

Use a stretch stitch on the machine. Back stitch only if sewing by hand. Note in the smallest bears, hand stitching is far more accurate and takes no longer. In the larger bears it takes a lot longer, but is still much more precise. In short you do not need a machine for this just needle thread pins and scissors.

Stretch fabrics will give a softer cuddlier bear. Make sure that they are machine washable however. Safe in Napisan and similar laundry soakers is also important if giving to children.

Make sure that the widest stretch of the fabric is aligned across the bear not top to bottom.

The maximum stretch is from left arm to right arm.

SOFT FURRY, VELVET, PANNE VELVET, FAUX FUR, CORDUROY AND SATIN.

All these fabrics have a stroke. Imagine that you are stroking a cat or dog. If you stroke from head to tail it is a lovely sensation for you and the pet. If you stroke in the opposite direction or crosswise, both you and the pet will not be happy, you may get scratched or worse.

Feel your fabric, stroke it in all four directions, up, down left and right. One direction will be beautiful, soft and silky smooth. This is ideal for teddies. This direction is the stroke of the fabric. On dress patterns it is always indicated with an arrow showing the direction of stroke.

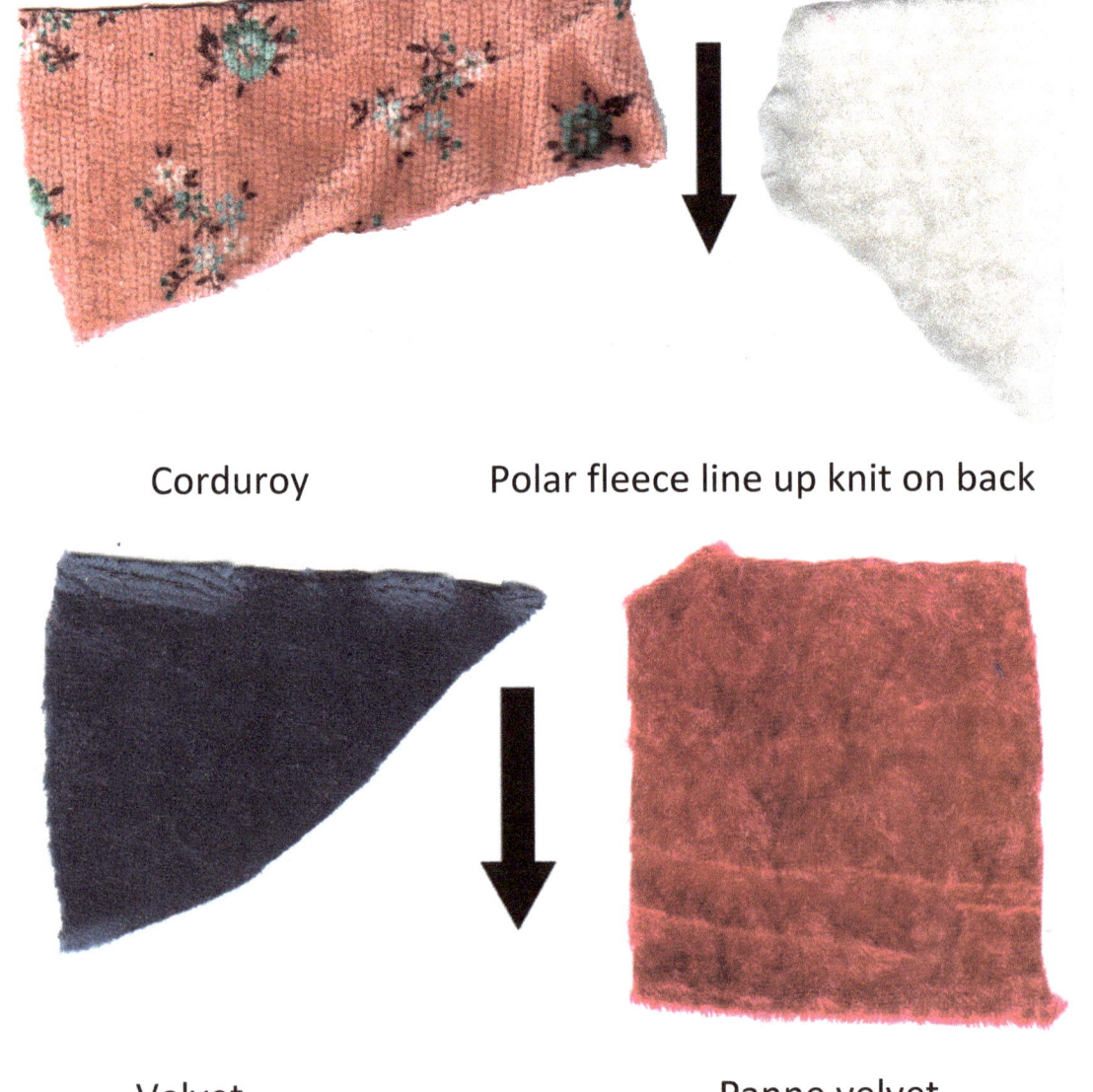

Corduroy　　　　　Polar fleece line up knit on back

Velvet　　　　　　Panne velvet

When laying out the pattern ensure that the stroke, like your pets is from head to toe. So easy to get a professional finish, get it wrong and even a 2 year old will reject it!

When sewing these fabrics they will move against each other when you sew them. Pin at right angles to sewing direction, then tack by hand with contrast thread and fairly large stitches. Remove the pins before final sewing.

Sew slowly.

Satin, if using the machine follow above directions and if a piece of test fabric moves, put toilet paper (unused of course) on the machine bed under the fabric. Magic! Then tear off paper after stitching. I used this technique on wedding dresses to save puckering on the older and more basic sewing machines.

Faux fur showing distinct stroke

Faux fur has a really thick pile (the length of the hairs). A good rule of thumb is for really tiny bears finished size 8cm or less don't use fur, instead use velvet, velour, panne velvet or pinwale cord. For bears 8cm to 12cm use short pile for a luxurious finish. For larger bears you can use slightly longer pile. Be very aware of stroke direction.

When pinning out push the pile away from the seam towards the centre of the bear, so that it doesn't get cut short at the seam. Cut carefully and slowly with great accuracy. Before sewing, pin and brush the pile with your hand away from the edge of the pattern.

After clipping the curves and turning right side out, gently pick out the hairs caught in the seam with a pin. This will allow the fur to cover the seam entirely.

Dressing up Basic Bear

Just a few simple things can suggest a personality.

For allergic children the basic bear in plain cotton is safest. I have used scraps of yellow spot to make it more cheerful. Note that plain cottons without the polyester for stretch or knit styles will wrinkle a little at curves, by the time that they are well cuddled this is not noticeable.

Cotton fabric non stretch

Cotton fabric with a 20cm length of satin ribbon gathered at the waist, with a short piece folded as bodice. A piece of lace or net can be gathered into fairy wings.

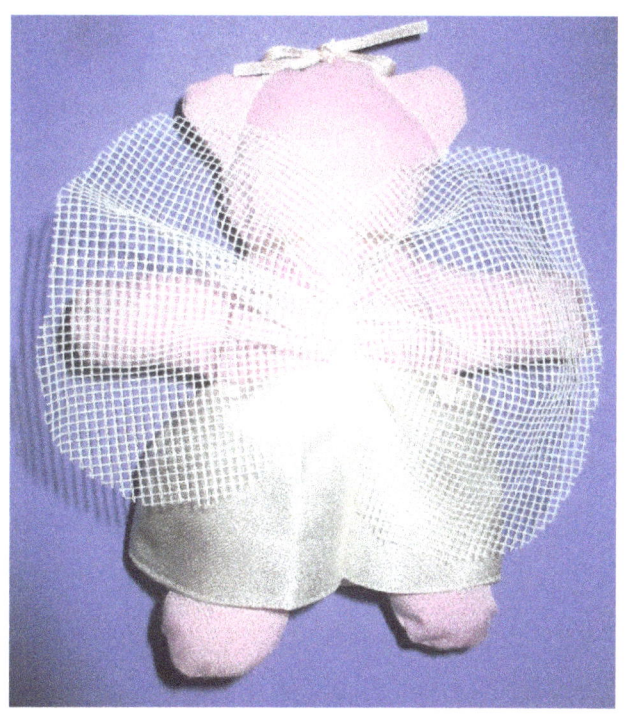

The following is a white polar bear made out of polar fleece, I have used the same bear just changed the accessories to turn it into, bride, groom, and biker. Have fun!

Polar bear in polar fleece

With polar fleece there is no stroke but be very careful to make sure that if it has a knit back is from top to bottom like the knit pattern on a jumper, some polar fleece is fluffy on both sides, no wrong side or stroke, jackpot! This bear has wobbly eyes, fabric paint details and a satin ribbon bow. With polar fleece it is necessary to trim the fleece on the face so that the fabric paint sticks to the fabric not the fleece. With embroidery this is not the case unless the fleece is very thick.

To turn this bear into a bride a little lace or net gathered on top of the head with tiny flowers or beads, some lace or satin ribbon for the dress and a bouquet if wished. I have used small pearl trim as a necklace. I have not cut the lace, nor sewn it down as the bear is about to be the groom. This is a great present, though I would suggest caramel colour polar fleece rather than white for the contrast.

Polar fleece bride

For the groom I used narrow black satin ribbon and a short piece of 3cm wide elastic, rounded the end, and dotted buttons in fabric paint.

You could make a little top hat out of cardboard or felt to finish it off. But often the simplest suggestions work best.

Bride groom in polar fleece

My favourite is the little bikie or biker bear. He is very popular with adults especially in the smaller sizes.

Bikie bear is transformed by using a bit of agricultural plastic or similar reasonably heavy duty black plastic.

Measure round the bear's finished torso plus just a little to overlap. Now cut a U shape at each arm deep enough so that the plastic overlaps the shoulders. Put a cross stitch in black on the shoulders. Now trim the back in a slight curve down at the back of the neck. Cut a V at the front. Use a liquid correction pen to do a logo. I used lightning bolt and initials BB for bikie bear. Either put a few stitches in the front of the vest or leave it open. For the bandanna a small triangle of fabric long enough to tie at the back and wide enough to just fold at the front. Now add a safety pin through the ear. For adults only.

Bikie bear in polar fleece

The bear can be in football colours, dressed as a member of a club, in offcuts of favourite clothes, it is limited only by your imagination.

Bears should be fun not serious, they are designed to be loved, played with and to show love. If your first attempt ends in tears, bin it and try another day. It is worth noting that my mother's first attempt at a bear was so misshapen that she called him Fuji, because he looked like he had survived the bombing at Hiroshima. My brother would not let her throw him out. He turned out to be my brother's favourite bear. If you have children nearby, anyone over seven could try to make their own, they may be starting a craft for life.

Bear in Various Sizes

Scale the patterns up or down using a photocopier, adults tend to prefer the pattern 16cm high, it is very cute and ideal for a mascot or keepsake. This is however the hardest to do, turning very tiny corners. I would leave this size for your fourth or fifth attempt, it is also the most difficult to turn and stuff. This pattern has a finished size of 13cm.

The mid-sized 19.5 cm pattern is still on the cute side but is easier to sew, turn and stuff. I recommend this as the first attempt for an adult who sews. This size is 16cm tall when complete. This is the size of pattern at the beginning of this chapter.

Photocopy the pattern and scale A4 to A3 this will give you the largest manageable size for this pattern. Any larger and the pattern distorts. This size is ideal for a young child's toy, and for a child or non-sewing adult to try for a first attempt. This size is easier to turn corners, stuff and decorate.

The following photo shows the medium and small bear together, you will note that the smaller bear in cotton wrinkles in the folds, had it been made in stretch, such as the panne velvet rose pink bear shown earlier this would not have been the case. Remember, no synthetic panne velvet and the like for allergy sufferers until you check.

Small and medium sized bears

The simple two piece bears are fun, but three piece, shaped bears are even nicer. Apart from lavender sachets, I no longer use the two piece pattern, this is because with a little extra effort and confidence you get a much nicer bear with a shaped nose and podgy belly.

This picture shows two bears made with the same fabric and decoration, one uses two pieces, one three. They are both cute and cuddly, both will be well loved. Once you master two piece bears, try three piece. The more pieces in the bear, the more detail and shaping that is possible. Commercial patterns would use between four and ten pieces for the head alone.

Book three shows you how to do the three piece bear with patterns.

Book 3:

Shaped Grizzly/Polar Bear

This is a very simple bear if you take it slowly, as you practise you can get faster. It takes only marginally more fabric and stuffing than the basic bear but looks 100% better because of the shaping.

Children love them as much as the adults. I would say that at least half of the bears that I have made live with adults.

Materials:

Fabric sufficient for two fronts and one back

Polyester or Dacron fibre fill

Embroidery thread or fabric paint, in black

Instructions:

Trace around the patterns in this book using greaseproof paper or photocopy just the pattern. If you are using the digital version print out these pages only. Note these patterns are copyright, therefore you may not use the patterns to make toys for a profit, nor may you give a copy of the pattern to a friend without permission. Contact us info.felixpublishing@gmail.com before you do. We may say yes!

Copy the small bear pattern A4 to A3 on a photocopier to get big teddy size. Small teddy and medium teddy are full sized. Copying Medium bear A4 to A3 will get a huge bear but it tends to lose shape if you go bigger.

Small bear front and back

Medium bear back pattern

Medium bear front pattern

Make sure the fabric is all facing the same way. If it has a stroke, the stroke must go from the head to toe of bear or you will be very sad.

Note at the top of the leg the pattern goes out, this is the seam width. Lay out the pattern, cut one back. Now fold the fabric right sides together, pin out the front and cut straight through both layers. Done.

Remove the patterns and pin the two fronts together. Make sure that the right sides are facing each other on the inside. Double check this, I cut 2 left sides making this it is easily done. Stitch fronts together leaving opening of at least 3 cm to stuff, in the belly.

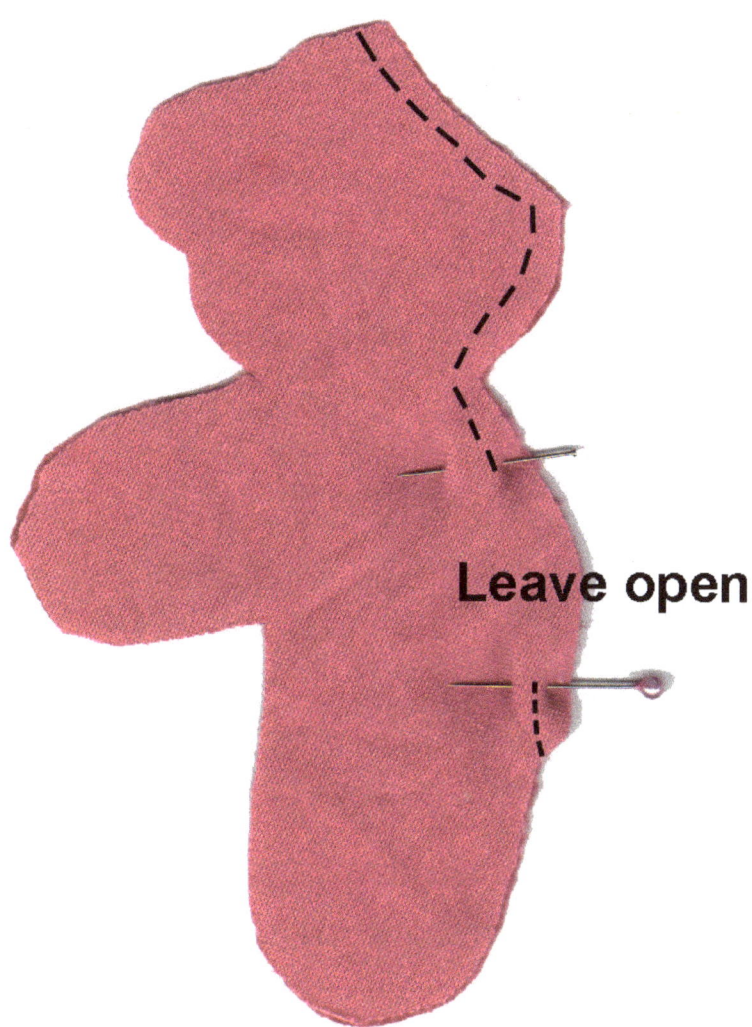

Front stitching lines, note the width.

Matching ears, feet and arms lay front on the back. Make sure that the right sides are inside. Pin at right angles to the seam.

If you are using fur fabrics, satin, velvet or velour, tack the seam in a contrasting colour. This will make it easier to remove later.

Clip the curve in the neck of front pieces, avoid cutting the seam open.

Pinning front to back.

Hand or machine stitch with the same seam width as the front, right around the outside. Do not leave any gaps on the outside for stuffing.

Remove the tacking and pins.

Clip the seams on all inside curves up to the stitching line. Check to see if neck centre seam was done. Be very careful not to cut the seams.

Now turn the whole bear inside out, carefully, use the blunt end of a pencil to push out ears, hands and feet. Roll the seams between your fingers to ensure the seams are fully turned.

Now carefully sew across the base of the ears.

Carefully stuff the bear. Order really does matter, if you do not follow the order you will not be able to stuff the extremities after the middle is stuffed.

Stuff the head first, then the arms, do not stuff belly. Stuff the legs one at a time, now stuff the belly. Use that pencil to smooth the stuffing to give a sleek surface on the outside. Do not leave gaps.

Ear stitching line at back of teddy

Carefully pin the sides of the belly making sure the seam width is constant. Use ladder stitch to finish the seam. Well done.

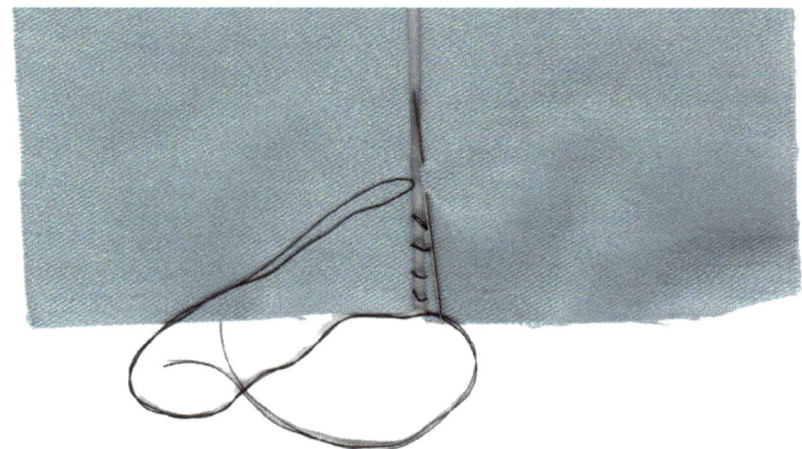

Ladder stitch.

Polar fleece bear

Polar fleece has very little stretch and is very easy to handle, this is ideal for beginners who want a good finish. It also has the bonus of fluff with no stroke. Just line up the ribbing on the back vertically. Polar fleece is very hard to turn right way out due to its thickness, go slowly and leave a longer opening for turning. Best for medium or large bear.

Panne velvet bear overstuffed.

Panne velvet has a strong stretch horizontally at right angles to the stroke. It has a beautiful finish always looks lovely and can take anything that a child or washing machine can give. To use this well, *only lightly stuff* or it will distort sideways and be useful as a warning for weight watchers. I deliberately overstuffed this pink panne velvet so that the distortion was visible. With lots of cuddling it will return to normal bear shape.

Long Fur Pile- Hairy Bear

If you are using fleece or fur pile, use scissors to trim the fur around the snout and eyes so that you can glue, stitch or paint the features. Observe other bears, they always do this or have the snout as a separate piece with shorter pile. The wobbly eyes are not for children under 3.

When doing the face, do one side of the face first, then turn the bear upside down to do the other side to match. Porcelain artists use this technique all the time as we tend to do a better job on one side due to being left or right handed.

A good rule of thumb is the smaller the bear the smaller the pile of plush fabric, and the shorter the pile of fur, and the smaller the detail of print fabrics. The fabric of the Hairy Bear would normally be used for a larger bear.

A long fur pile bear like this with wobbly eyes is definitely for children over 3, do not be tempted ever, to give it to younger children. You can neatly brush the fur so that he looks more refined like on the right leg, but I deliberately scruffed him up to make him look scary. Your choice, as soon as the photo was taken his right leg was scruffed.

Now to decorate. This is the really fun part.

Once you have done one or two and are confident you can cut out a few at once. This is especially true at Christmas.

Note when using multiple layers make sure that you can see the edges of each so that you are not disappointed that red ted has no nose and green ted has only half a leg. Making harlequin bears allows you to use those long thin scraps from where you cut out sleeves that are too thin for use elsewhere. Remember you need only one back for every two fronts. Basic bear needs less fabric but is less exciting.

Styling Your Unique Bear, Wedding/Bikie/Floral/Christmas

When making a bear for children 8 months and younger (before they start crawling), avoid long pile fur and panne velvet as these tend to lose very fine fibres in the first week or so. These fibres may trigger a cough or asthma, not always, but it could happen. If the child is crawling, do not worry, as a child health nurse once told me, once the baby crawls they will eat dirt, fluff and cockroaches in the cleanest house, so forget sterilising bottles. The children become hardier after this. I usually let them choose the fabric from that age on. That said keep young children's bears simple, they prefer it and there are fewer things for them to pull off and swallow/ choke on.

NEVER PUT EYES, BUTTONS, NOSES, PINS, PLASTIC on any bear for a child under 3. You must either embroider or paint them on. Even the child-safe non-removable eyes can be removed by dextrous and determined children who just have to try. I have seen it. Under 3 children explore their surroundings with their mouth before their eyes and hands, older children use hands first because of their increasing dexterity. It is bad enough taking a child to the ambulance station to have peas removed from his nose well pushed in (this took less that a second to insert, but an hour to remove and we were next to him as he did it), something harder such as eyes could prove fatal and you would not see him do it if he was in his cot. I am not sexist, just the mother of sons, therefore my examples are male.

If you are selling your bears to raise money for a charity, assume that they will be bought for children under 3 by devoted grandparents. If you want the beautiful child-safe or special teddy bear eyes and noses, put the bear in a plastic bag with warnings on the bag and pinned to the bear.

Christmas Bears are such fun, and very popular with all ages. Use the smallest bear pattern and use reds, greens, white or a combination of these. Use scraps of Christmas themed fabric, or just add a tartan ribbon in red/green.

Red bear with tartan tie

Harlequin style with opposite sides of the body in different colours are very popular, it is also a great way to use up scraps. Warning here, make sure that the right sides are facing before you cut them out or you will end up with two right sides or two left. To avoid this use plain fabric with no right and wrong side. Simple!

Harlequin bear

Some love to use them as decorations round a room, on the table or hanging on the tree. For decorations on the tree, fold a 10cm length of ribbon, insert the cut ends into the head seam before sewing round the outside. If someone wants to turn a bear that is finished into a tree bear, do not panic. Get thick knitting yarn in a darning needle, sew once through the top of the bear at the centre seam, and tie a knot in the thread making a loop. Voila! It is done. You could also use fine silver chord that is used for wrapping presents.

Decoration bear for trees etc.

Plain colours of inexpensive cotton for your Christmas bears eliminate the need for right side and wrong side of fabrics. When buying red, green and white get them before November as those three colours sell out fast towards Christmas when the special seasonal prints come in. Plain lawn can be as low as $2 per metre but seasonal prints are around $15 - $25. Similarly the fibre filling goes up towards Christmas every year. Fabric stores tend to have a monopoly on stuffing most of the year, they take advantage of this with higher prices. Around Christmas discount department stores such as Kmart and Big W, also stock stuffing suitable for cuddly toys, watch for specials. A specialist bear or doll store will sell much firmer stuffing suitable for the hard bears collectors are fond of. If you graduate to these bears, they have up to thirty individual pattern pieces, delicately shaped that look magnificent. Sadly most are not very cuddly. You will need to get very specific fabrics as well as jointing. For these simple patterns the softer polyester fill is more suitable and cuddly. If you cannot easily source the fill and have an old pillow, wash it in disinfectant and dry it in the sunshine. When the pillow is dry use the middle parts for stuffing the outer section is too stiff and will warp your bear.

Tiny print Christmas bear.

For the following variations I will use the polar bear pictured earlier so that you can clearly see the difference a few trims can make.

Wedding Bears are really cute for putting on the bridal table, if you are lucky you might get a tiny piece of the wedding dress fabric from the maker, this is indeed a very special keepsake, especially if the wedding dress is hired, or given to someone else or borrowed. This is good economically and environmentally.

Bride and groom made from polar bears pictured earlier.

Tiny bears are best for this. I used medium bears to make photography easier. To copy a satin dress get wide satin ribbon, for a crossover dress put strips of ribbon over the shoulder and cover by using another strip of ribbon round the legs. Use tiny hand stitches to hold it in place. If you have trimmings from a lace curtain that works really well. For the bouquet tiny artificial flowers sewn to the right hand look lovely. Veil, if worn is netting or lace, think cheap curtaining sample, gather at the short side on to the top of the head, and stitch it on. Sew a few tiny beads or artificial flowers on the top.

Groom is usually simple to make. Black satin bow tie and white bib with tiny black dots for buttons. If you use a larger bear it is possible to actually make the whole suit and wedding dress but mostly this would be too big for the table. The idea is to suggest the idea and just choose the defining items to put on the bear. Too much fuss is never good.

Groom vest full sized pattern

Bikie Bear is by far the favourite of adults. He is so cute and the antithesis of a scary gang member. Again suggestion is the way to go. NEVER DO THIS FOR A YOUNG CHILD. Use black agricultural plastic, or thick black bin bags if you use them to make the jacket. Measure a rectangle the width of the waist on your finished bear (15cm + 2mm for tiny cotton bear) this varies on how you stuffed the bear and if there is a pile on the fabric, and the height of the base of the jacket to the shoulder plus 2mm (5.5 cm +.2cm for cotton tiny bear). Wrap the long side round your bear and do a vertical cut halfway down at the seam of the arm on both sides. Now measure the width of the finished arm seam, carefully cut a U with 1cm either side of the cut. Shape a V at the front. I have included the pattern for a cotton bear you will need to scale it up for fur pile. Polar fleece next page next to cotton bear.

Polar fleece waistcoat   cotton bear waistcoat

Put a cross stitch joining the front shoulder to the back shoulder on both sides. Using liquid paper or similar do a logo suitable for your bear. If you have a cheap piece of broken chain, stitch it either side of the fronts. Put a small safety pin through the ear as an ear ring. You can also put one through the eyebrow. Make bandanna if wished.

Now give him a sweet face and smile.

Bikie Jacket full sized pattern cotton bear.

For polar fleece use larger waistcoat pattern and just trim lower edges to match.

Floral Bear is a fun bear using the prettiest floral fabric that you can find. Maybe a child's favourite dress that no longer fits or is stained and worn out. A keepsake or memory or someone that you love. A favourite shirt of someone who has recently passed away will be valued for years. Take extra special care of this one, maybe use the shirt buttons as eyes. Rosemary in the stuffing for remembrance would also go well. No photo here, it is your keepsake.

Bean Bag Bears use any of the patterns and simply stuff loosely with rice. The ideal fabrics are old curtaining or thick winter fabrics to take the beating when these are thrown. Double stitching is a good idea as well, they will be thrown after all.

This is the tiniest bear with medium pile fur fabric, he is sturdy and fun ideal for an adult present any time of the year.

Book 4:

Simple Dolls

Once you have made a simple 2 piece bear the rest is fairly straight forward. These have extra pattern pieces to allow more variety.

The doll is a top and bottom same for front and back. There is a waist seam that is left partly open at the back for turning. These are the traditional rag dolls. Originally they were made from salvageable fabric from worn through sheets, and the clothes from old clothes beyond salvaging. The original stuffing would have been old rags or kapok from the old fashioned heavy pillows.

Amish people did not put faces on as it was seen as making an idol, expressly forbidden in the Bible. Whether you put a face on or not is your choice. Faceless dolls are popular as are dolls with huge faces like Japanese cartoons, or those closer to normal proportions.

Fabric paint, embroidery or stitch on eyes are all options for older children and adults.

For children under 3 years old, embroidered, painted or blank are your choices. Safety is paramount for the little ones. Softer fabrics are preferred by the littlies.

If you are making the doll in pyjamas or nightie paint the face or embroider with eyes closed.

The pattern on the next pages can be scaled up on a photocopier, or scaled down on a scanner at home. Make sure if you do this both pieces are the same scale.

I suggest that you do 2 photocopies of each pattern onto coloured paper if you have it. Then cut around the pattern with your preferred seam allowances.

Keep one as the master copy and do the adjustments on the other, this way you have the original.

If you are using scraps, very sensible, it may be awkward to get both top pieces on the fold. This is true if they are on differing sections of the fabric.

Get another piece of paper and use sticky tape (Sellotape or Durex depending on country) to exactly line up the edge of the paper with the fold line on the front. Add seam allowances all round and cut out. When you open it up you will have a pattern for the whole top.

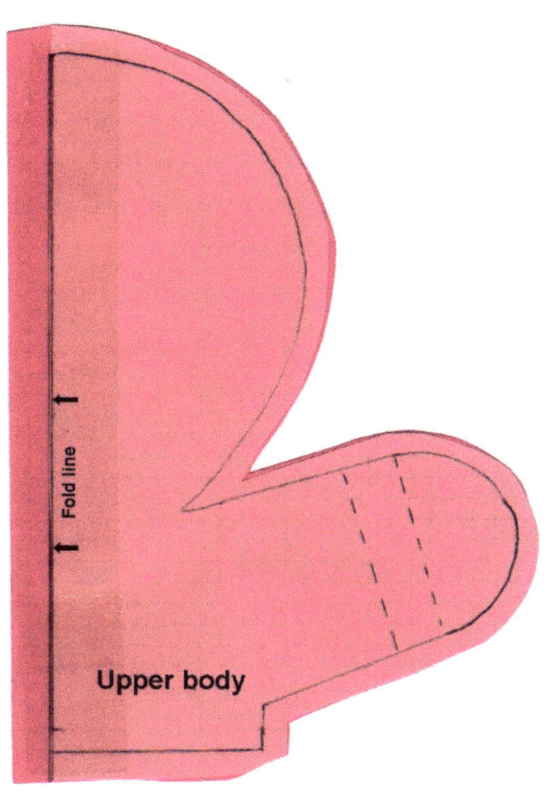

Two layers of pattern stuck together

Below pattern opened out

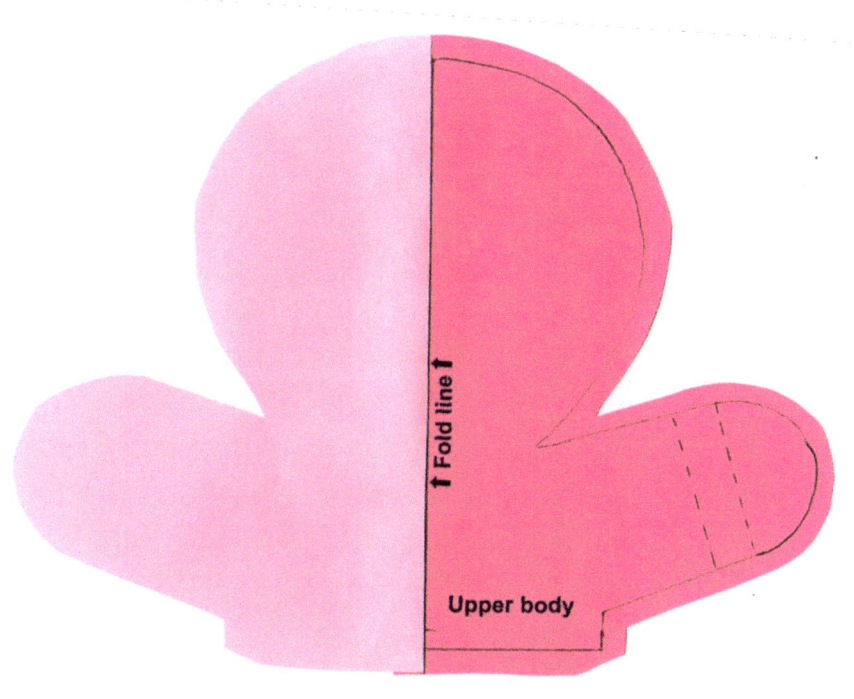

Doll, bear, rabbit, mouse

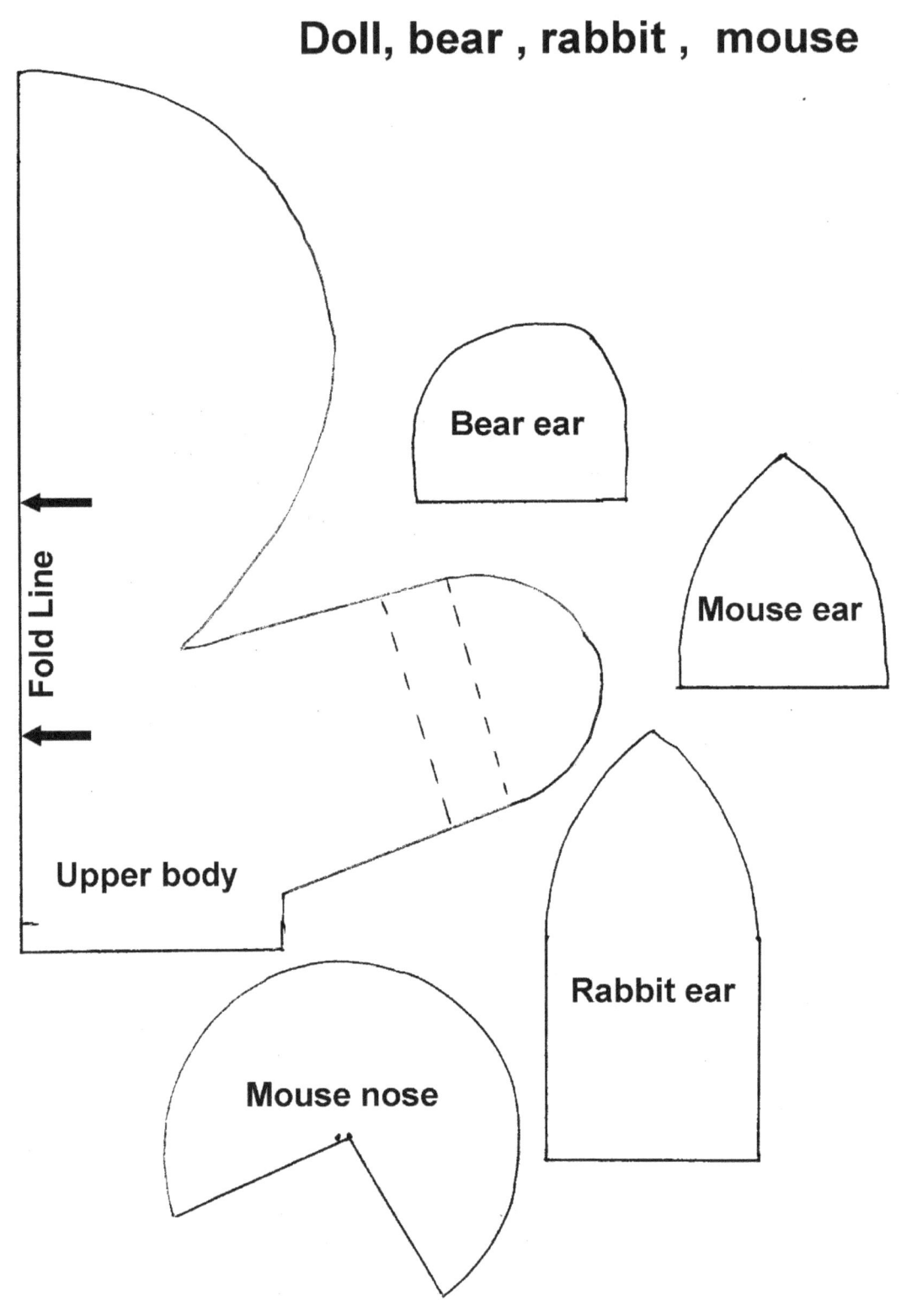

These patterns have no seam allowances the line is the stitching line, make sure you leave 2-3mm all-round except at fold.

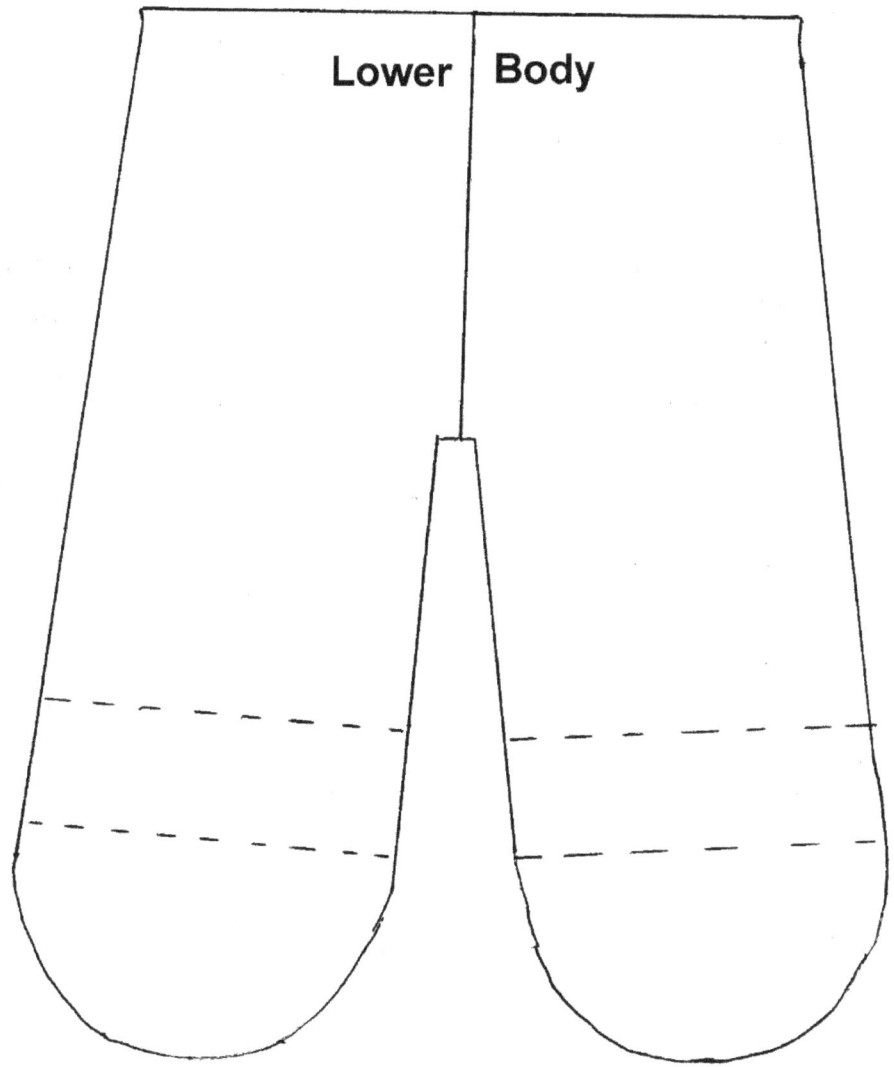

All patterns are full size but you can scale them as you wish

Patterns are for three sizes, coloured ones are for smaller sizes.

When I make the doll in onesies I cut the pattern at the neck and add seam allowances on both pieces. It is easier to cut out the fabric if all the adjustments have been made on the pattern. I then cut out two lower bodies and one total upper body and one half of the upper body in pyjama fabric. I then cut the face out of skin tone. You can make two face pieces if you want to put hair on the back of the head, great for curls, plaits (braids) or ponytails.

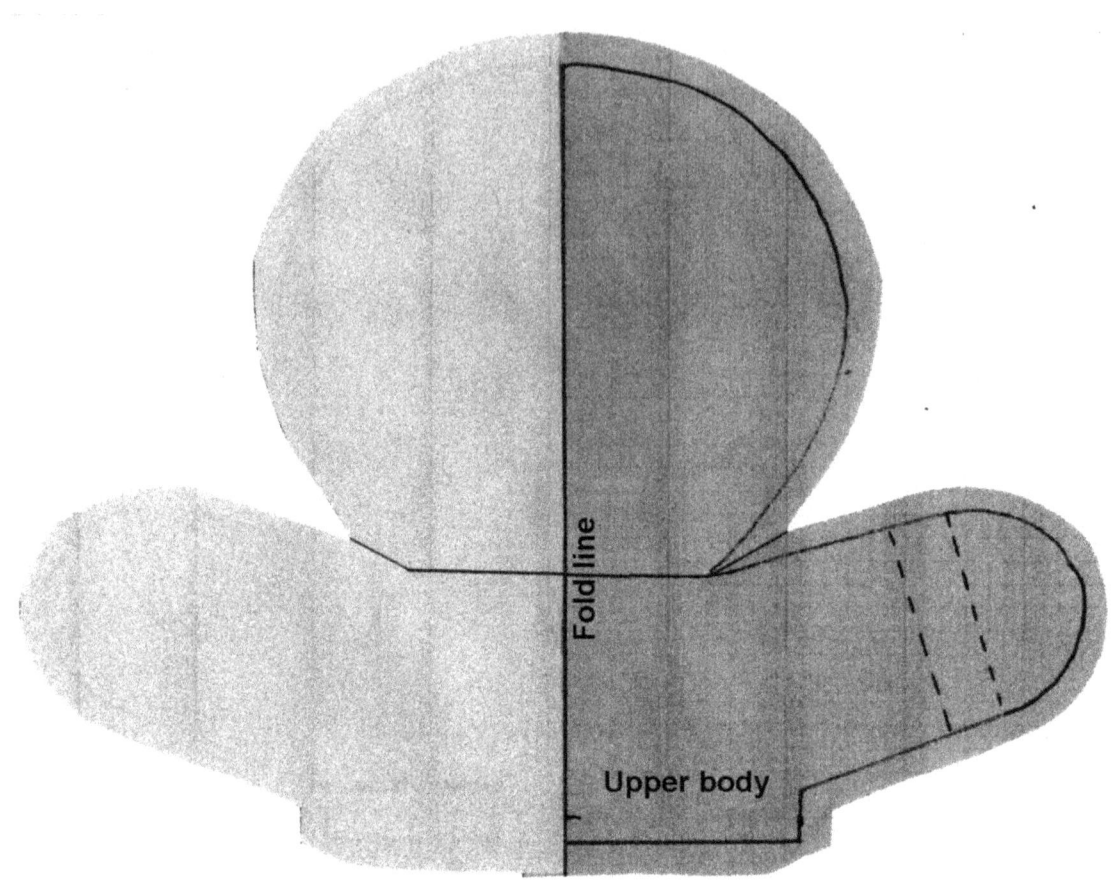

Upper body marked ready to separate

For a onesie doll cut out one the above top in pyjama material, and two of the lower body in pyjama material, then the lower top on the next page also in pyjama material. Now cut out the face from the next page in skin colour of choice.

The lay out is shown on the following pages.

You can do front and back with head separate, then join the patterns for the lower top and bottom with sticky tape ready to do it in one piece below the neck.

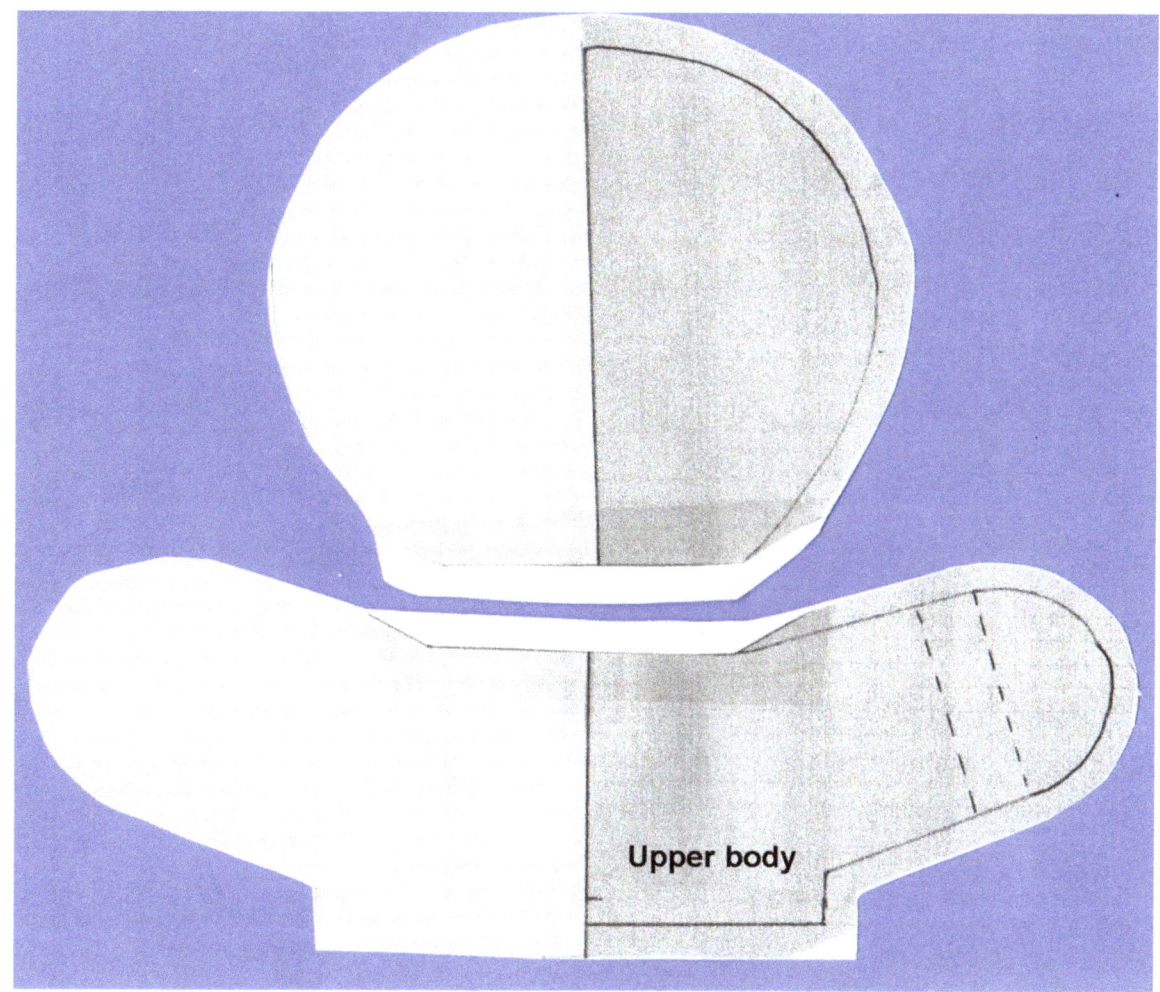

Basic Doll.

Materials:

25 cm of 112 cm wide fabric in skin colour of choice

Oddments of fabric for clothes Shorts 15cm x 30cm

T shirt 30cm x 60 cm

Dress 27cm x 40cm

Polyester or Dacron fibre fill

25 g acrylic yarn for hair

Embroidery threads or fabric paint

Method:

Cut out 2 lower bodies. Cut 2 upper bodies both on the fold, or if you adjusted the pattern just 2 total upper bodies. If you like long arms and legs adjust the patterns by lengthening at the dotted lines. If you do the whole thing in skin colour then you can easily dress the doll, or the child can later.

Pin top to bottom at waist on back, do the same for the front. Keep right sides facing each other.

Sew 2cm in from both sides at the waist on the back. Leaving a gap to stuff. Sew straight across the waist at the front.

Cut strip cardboard (old toilet rolls work) 8cm x 2 cm

Wind the yarn round the short side until it is covered. Sew near the edge.

Stitched fringe

Very carefully tear away the cardboard to leave just the yarn and stitching.

This is ready to insert in the seam at the top of the head.

Long fringes look great.

Onesie doll back   Onesie doll front

Layout of onesie doll with contrast face.

To put long or curly hair at the back cut out two sets of the front layout.

For those new to sewing toys always start with the largest size first. The medium doll is cute but harder to sew, the small doll is only for the very patient, accurate or experienced person.

The large doll is ideal for sporting mascots the two piece body to be in team colours, cut out two sets of fronts and put long hair or curls on the back of the head.

Doll sizes complete: Large doll 12 ½ inches, 34 cm; Medium doll 6 ½ inches, 16cm; Tiny doll 11.5cm, 4 ½ inches.

Medium doll one colour

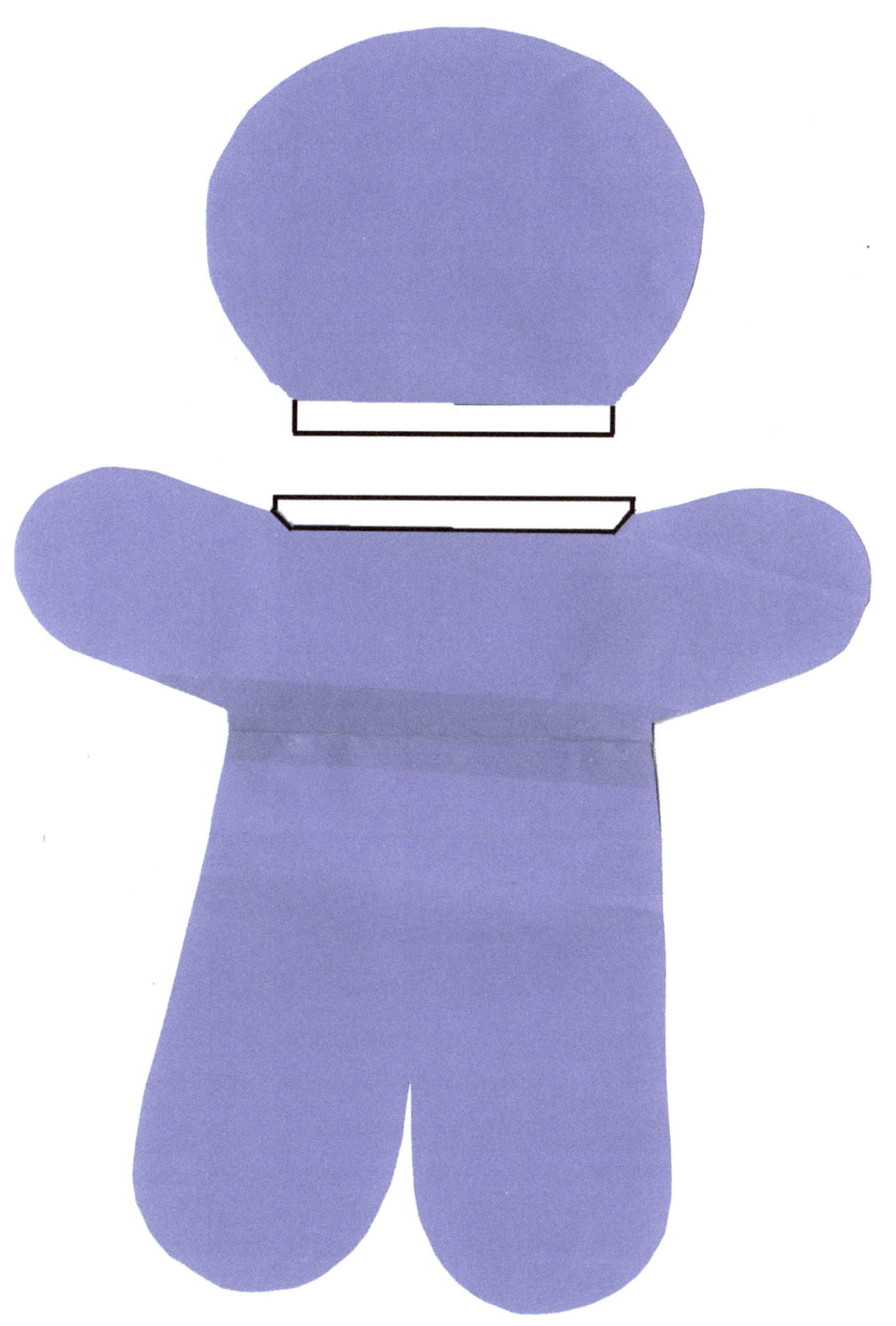

Medium doll head separate colour

Small doll pattern

The easiest way to make the small dolls is to sew round the head but not the neck, sew around the body but not neck. Turn right side out. Hand sew front of neck to front of body. Stuff doll, then ladder stitch the back of the neck. Sew on hair if desired after completion.

To do the hair, either wind the yarn around cardboard as pictured earlier and sew it into the head seam or loop it evenly over the head seam after the long hair is stitched on.

To do long hair wind the long hair over a tray or similar to get the right length. You will need the length of the hair from the end of the pony tail up and over the head and down to the end of the pony tail on the other side. Add another 10 cm for stretching. Now keep winding until you have the width to be covered from the top of the head to the bottom of hairline. Carefully remove the loops of yarn, marking the centre with a pin. Pin this to centre front of head. Carefully oversew taking the strands about 6-8 at a time, continue in a straight line down the back making the part.

Tie the hair into pony tails at the side, add fringe in tiny loops now.

For plaits (braids) allow 50% extra length in the winding to get the plaits as long as you wanted.

Paint or embroider face after hair is done.

All clothes patterns are for the **largest** doll pattern, use photocopier to scale down for other sizes.

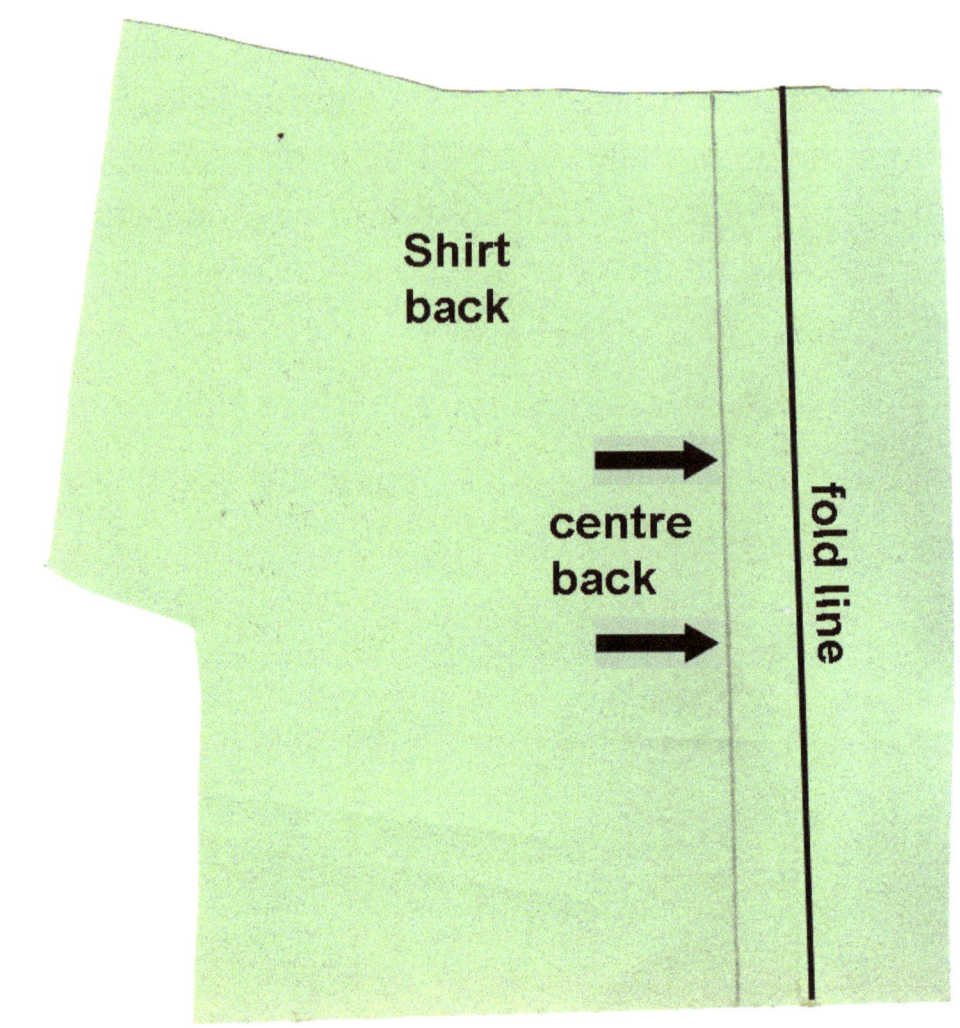

Shirt back cut two

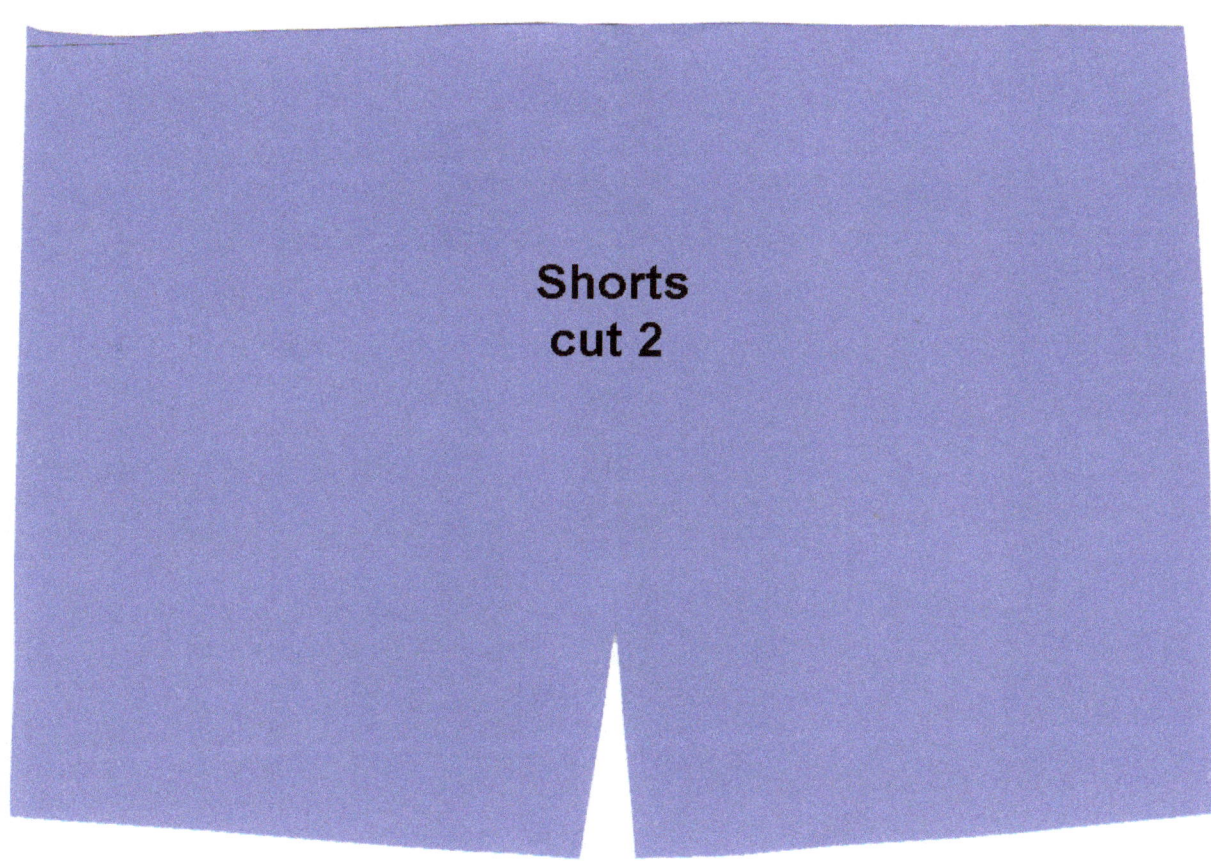

Shorts, for large doll

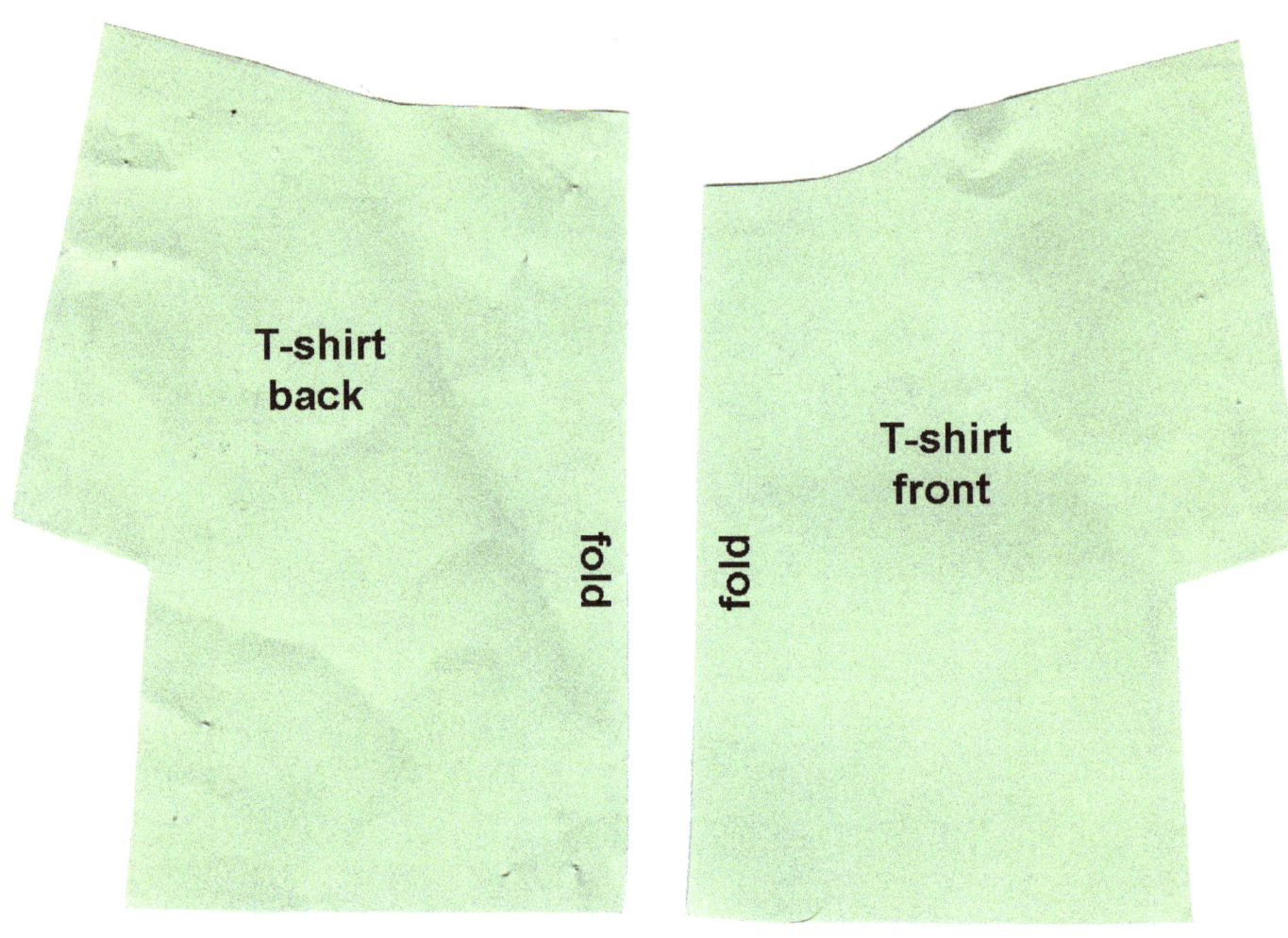

T-shirt, T-shirt front is also shirt front.

To make t-shirt:

Use stretch fabric, cut out one front and one back on the fold. 3mm seams allowed.

Sew shoulders together, fold under 3mm and hem neck. Fold under 3mm at sleeve ends and hem. Sew arm/side seam. Hem bottom.

To make shirt:

Cut out t-shirt front on fold, and two shirt backs with right sides facing.

Sew shoulder seams. Sew neck hem and sleeve hem. Now sew side arm/ body. Fold backs at fold line, and hem. Hem bottom of shirt.

Add press studs or Velcro to the back matching centre back. Neatening of seams in doll clothes is usually only done for extremely detailed and heirloom dolls, suit yourself, but be aware that a child under 5 is likely to strip the removable clothes and never put them back on.

Dress pattern cut 2

Dress:

Cut 2 pieces, for extra gathering make the pattern wider by about 6-8 cm. 3mm seams are allowed.

Sew side seams, then sew round both arm holes. Hem the bottom, add lace or frill if desired.

Fold over top hem, at the line, stitch then thread elastic or ribbon through the front then continue to the back. Ribbons with bows at each shoulder look cute but leave them for the over fives. Elastic is best for the younger ones and saves frustration.

Shorts:

Cut two in any fabric. For undies just shorten the legs to almost nothing.

With right sides facing sew side seams and crotch (inside leg) seam. Hem the legs. Fold over top hem, using a three step zigzag stitch slightly stretch elastic as you sew inside the hem. Hand sewing fold over and hem, then thread elastic through. Clip at right angles round crotch seam being careful not to cut the stitches.

Shirt and shorts on large doll

Small Doll:

When making small doll, I strongly suggest that you do it by hand. The corners are so tight and seams so narrow, that it is more likely the machine will take your doll down and chew it as it does not allow for narrow seams or starting close to the edge. If you use back stitch, it will not take you much longer than machine stitching, if the machine plays up it will be considerably longer to machine sew. If you are using stretch material the machine will eat it for sure. Eating is my description of the fabric and thread getting drawn down into the bobbin area, getting caught in the mechanism and giving you quality time digging it all out as you become familiar with how your machine operates. The up side of this is that your machine gets a good clean out and you oil it before putting it back together.

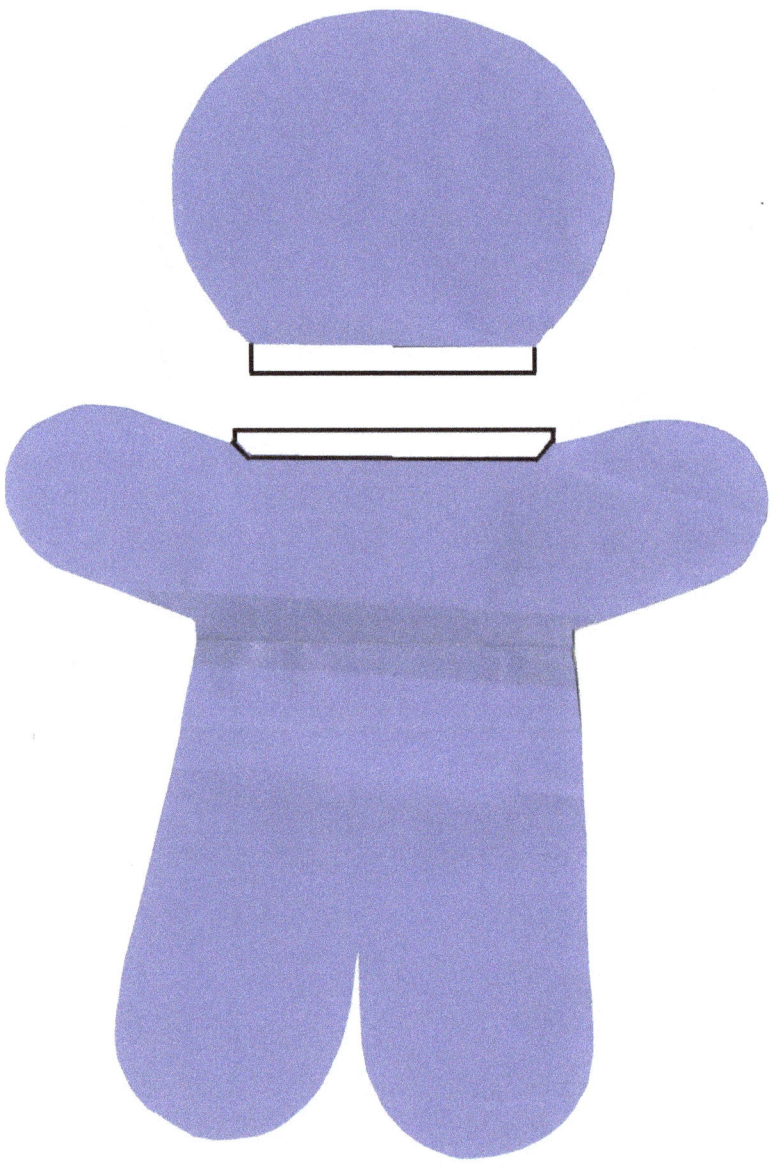

Small doll with head separate colour

Add extra length to neck to make it easier.

I have done the small doll in the traditional style of a waking/sleeping doll. These were very popular when children just had the one toy for life, not a new one bought just because you went shopping. I used stretch neutral fabric for the head and allowed extra length for tucking in at the neck. Stuffing is easier if the bottom pieces are sewn together with right sides facing, curves clipped then head stitched around. Stuff both pieces independently then pin and hand sew round the neck.

I looped the yarn for the hair and back stitched it across the head seam. I then plaited wool to stitch under the final loops.

Looping hair then backstitching

Decorate a sleeping face on one side and a waking face on the other. To get the soft effect on the cheeks, I used a red permanent marker, coloured in a folded tissue, then applied like rouge/ blusher. It must be permanent marker or it will wash off. I used a pin dipped into fabric paint to get the other tiny features and glued on wobbly eyes for the waking side.

Embroidered faces are beautiful and allow much room for creativity. Try these when you have mastered making and stuffing the dolls.

Two faced doll, full sized

Using Panne velvet feels lovely, wears well, but is very difficult to sew. Warning for newer toy makers. It could end in tears. Thin fabrics, cottons, old wool blankets are best for new toymakers as they give good results with less drama. Fabrics with a stroke, fur pile, or stretch are best after you have had a few successes. The stiffer the fabric, and less flexible the more difficult that it is to turn inside out. Larger sizes are recommended when using tactile fabrics with longer pile or stiffer backing.

Big doll with dress and shorts

No face Amish style

Simple Rabbits

To turn doll into rabbit cut around the rabbit ears pattern, two of the main colour and two of inside ear contrast. Stitch around the ears leaving short seam opened, turn them right side out.

Face lining of ears on the face of the rabbit.

Pin in place. Now sew as for doll.

Add fluffy pom pom to lower back.

Warning if you are using fabric that has a definite stroke, like a cat, make sure that the fabric is smoothest stroking from head to toe.

Tiny rabbit in Pane velvet

Cutting layout for rabbit

Simple Bears

Use the same pattern as the doll. All seams 3mm.

Cut out two ears in main fabric and two in lining.

Sew ears together with right sides facing, leave the lower edge open.

Turn the ears right side out.

Lay ear lining side on the face of the bear, pin the ears into position, then pin the rest of the bear together and follow instructions for the doll pattern that you have chosen.

Bear with no snout in cotton

Either stuff with pillow filling or uncooked rice for beanie bear.

You can leave the bear at that or you can add the snout for the mouse.

Bear with shaped snout

After stuffing the bear, sew the two straight sides of the snout together to make a cone, (mouse nose). Then sew across the point down .5 cm. Make sure seam is at the middle of the snout.

Turn right side out.

Lightly stuff the snout.

Turn under seam allowance and pin to front of face. Carefully oversew the snout to the face using thread to match the snout not the bear.

Now decorate the face, tie on a bow and you are done.

Layout for bear no snout cut ear in lining as well

Add mouse nose to this layout in fabric that matches ear lining to do bear with snout. Ensure that you have the rounded ear for bear and more pointed ear for mouse.

Simple Mouse:

As above for bear with snout but use pointier ears. You can shorten the ears by pushing them lower into the head before sewing. You can add a tail by rolling a length of the main fabric and over stitching it, or add a chord or bias binding folded over and stitched lengthwise. If it is for a young child leave off the tail it will be ripped off and present a choking hazard.

Mouse in cotton lawn

The cotton lawn is the easiest to sew and is ideal for allergic children, however the finish is nowhere near as nice as some of the other fabric.

Mouse pattern layout, cut extra ear in contrast

Once you have mastered these patterns try a commercial pattern with multiple pieces, I cannot show you pictures of these as it would be a breach of copyright. Sufficient to say, master the simple patterns first, then when you have confidence, borrow or buy a pattern of a toy that you really want to make, FOLLOW THE INSTRUCTIONS and go slowly. Success is assured if you follow instructions (work out short cuts only after success the first time), use the appropriate fabrics and stuffing, and go slowly.

Have fun! If you are not having fun and enjoying the fruits of your labour, try some other craft. I did all the toys in this book quickly so that they would look authentically like a first effort. Yes using these patterns I have made adorable and keepsake toys.

I designed these patterns to teach predominantly disengaged young teenage boys at a very challenging school. The boys got their photos in the paper as they proudly displayed their efforts. Their marks improved and self-esteem rocketed. They made some truly beautiful bears, they used the three piece bear in book three.

Book 5:

Bear Blankie (Baby Cuddle Blanket Square)

This style of comfort toy has become very popular in recent years, it is a combination of little bear and blanket square. As you will have already done the bears in books 2-4 this will be easy and very rewarding.

Pattern is full size.

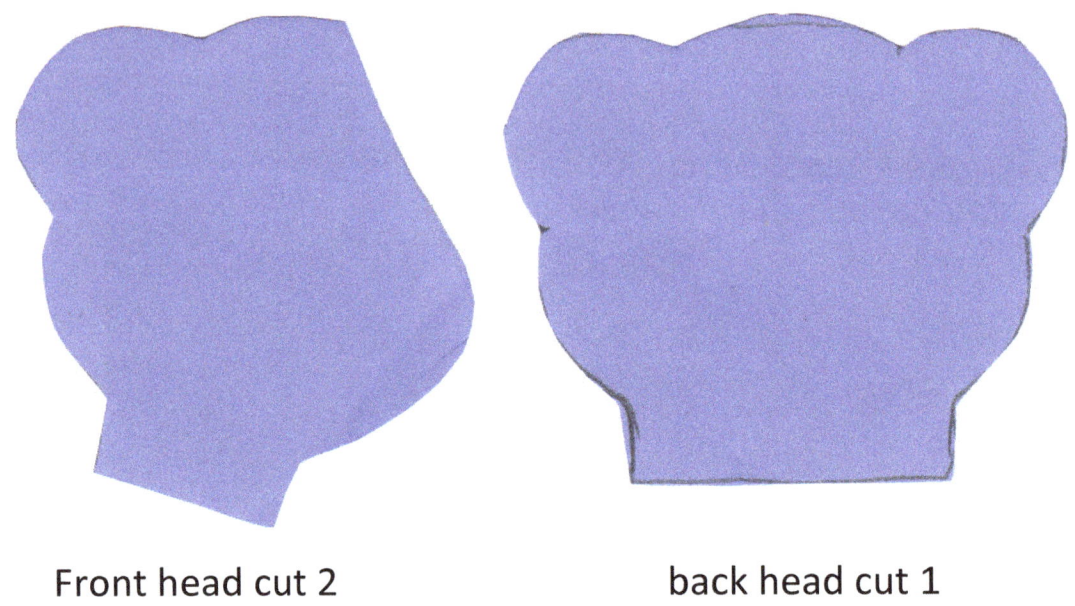

Front head cut 2   back head cut 1

Bear Blanket:

This is popularly known as a blankie. This is a very popular comforter or security blanket. Because this will be loved to pieces or ignored you need to be very careful with choices of fabric and decoration. All fabrics need to be able to be able to be machine washed, soaked in nappy soaker, durable and non allergic. All details, eyes, trims etc. also need to be painted, embroidered or heavily stitched. UNDER NO CIRCUMSTANCES USE STITCH ON OR CHILD SAFE EYES, or BUTTONS. Babies will choke, they will remove the decorations when you least expect it.

Materials:

27cm x 8 ½ cm head material

30cm x 30cm polar fleece or similar cuddly fabric, or plain cotton.

Hand full of polyester fill

Embroidery thread or fabric paint for details.

Method:

3 mm seams (1/4 inch) allowed on the pattern

Cut out two fronts right sides facing, one back of head, ensure stroke of fabric is from top to bottom of head.

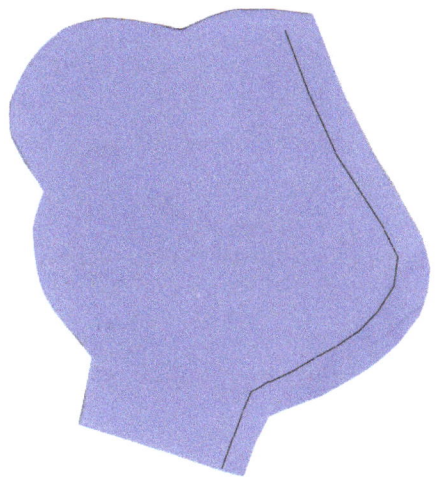

Front stitching line

Sew centre front seam from top to bottom, open out the seam before pinning to back of head. Right sides all together inside.

Stitch round the whole head from neck back to the neck being very careful with sharp and slow turns.

Clip all curves up to the seam line but not through the stitching.

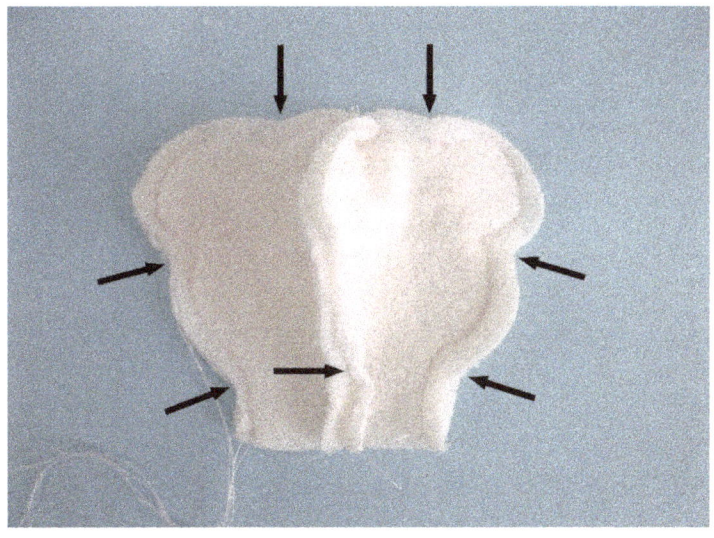

Arrows mark points to clip.

Turn the head right side out, being careful to press out ears with the blunt end of a pencil or similar.

Stitch across the base of the ears, conforming to the curve of the head in matching thread.

Stuff the head, not too firmly.

Cut the blanket out, 30cm x 30cm rounding the corners.

Using an overlocker make a rolled hem all round, or a tiny hem by hand or machine. Small firm stitches are needed for this, remember it will do as heavy duty as a pair of work jeans.

Fold the blanket diagonally twice to find the centre point.

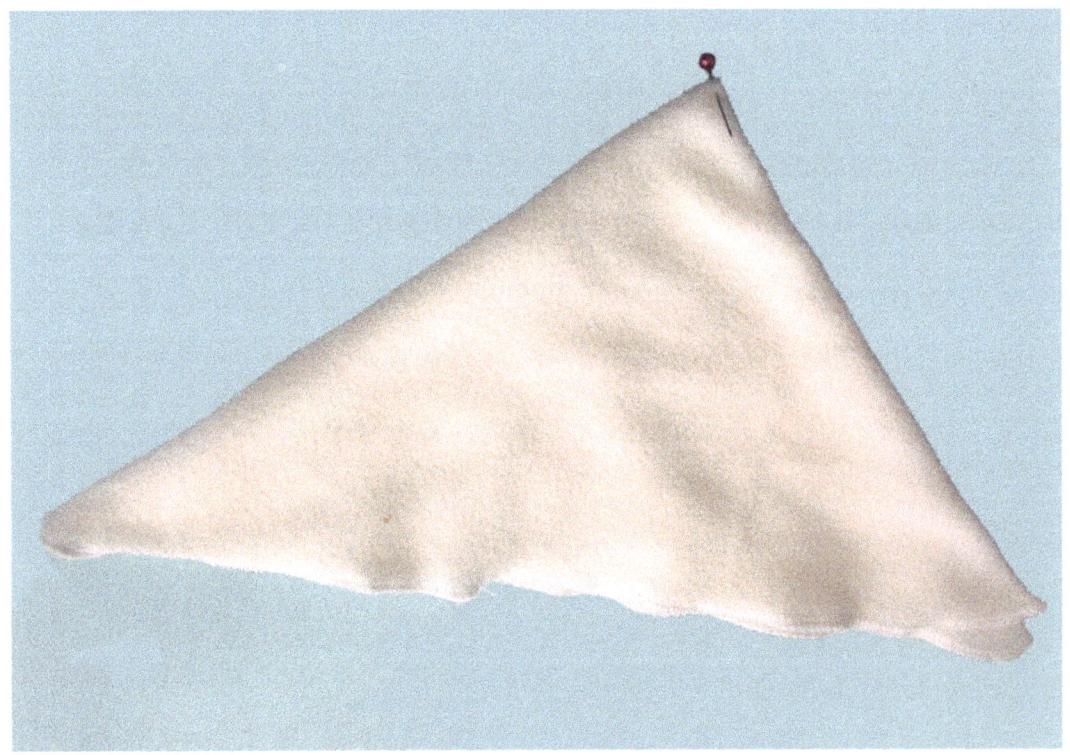

Centre point on folded blanket

Open the blanket out and lay it on a table. Pin the head, facing one of the corners, with ears aligned with opposite corners. Fold under the seam allowance to pin the head in place. With doubled thread matching the head, carefully, with tiny stitches oversew the head to the centre of the blanket.

Sew a bow or gathered lace, again to cover the seam, again very tiny stitches, very firmly. Tiny fingers get caught in big stitches, they also rip them out.

Now the fun bit, put on the face using embroidery or fabric paint, again do not glue or sew eyes, do not put on child safe eyes either, my children are not the exception in being able to remove them (you will be pleased to know that I caught them as they were doing it, and learned from it). The emergency department at the hospital will thank you for not using them. Child safe eyes are only for children over 3 on firmly stuffed traditional teddies using very heavy, close weave fabrics.

Two Blankies

Book 6:
Cubby House/Wendy House/Play House

Most children like somewhere to escape, hide or play quietly by themselves. When they are kept indoors because of ill health, the weather or apartment living, it is hard to build a cubby house outside. These designs are for a tent covering a table that is easily removable, washable and easy to store. Whilst you can go out and buy the fabrics to make this, old or stained sheets are ideal and most houses have at least one sheet in that category waiting to be upcycled.

Children can help design and decorate it.

Very basic cubby:

If you have a queen sized sheet and a small table, 1m x 1- 1½ m long, acrylic paints or contrast fabric you are ready to go.

Spread sheet over table, making sure it just touches the floor on the front and one side. It should overhang the other two sides.

The children are happy just playing with that. Maybe lift one side a little higher to let air in. Well done!

Now for the slightly more impressive version:

Spread sheet over table, if it is patterned put right side face down. Make sure it just touches the floor on the front and one side. It should overhang the other two sides.

Pull the corners out, and pin vertically from the corner of the table down to the floor, do this on all four corners. This should give you four nice even vertical sides.

Sheet pinned vertically at corners

Now carefully lift the sheet off the table. And sew from the table top down to the floor on three sides. Use overlocker to trim and strengthen the seams, or cut away the waste and zig zag over the raw edges.

On the fourth side just sew from the corner down 10 cm. Allow about 2cm beyond the pins for the seam and cut away the corners. Hem the opening. This is the children's entrance.

Put the cover back on the table and pin up the hem on the two sides that did not exactly touch the floor, so that they too touch the floor. Trim the hem to 2 cm then remove cover and stitch the hem.

Paint on door and windows, maybe even a garden and let it dry for 24 hours.

If you want to go more complex, cut out a window or two, neaten the edges, and make a flap out of the scraps to roll up.

If you have a folding card table, a single bed sheet and 1½ m of contrast fabric and a few trimmings from fly screens you can make the pictured cubby.

Cubby with door and windows sewn on

For people who are not confident in cutting fabric just laying over a table, those who are using synthetic fabrics or have polished / glass tables or who have children helping them, it is wise to carefully measure and mark out the pieces before cutting. In other words it is best to mark actual measurements on the diagram of the table then add the seam allowances and mark them on the patterns for the individual pieces.

Cutting diagrams are on the next page. I suggest that you copy that page and write the measurements directly onto the printout.

A cubby house such as this makes a great Christmas or birthday present. Parents enjoy watching the children have fun, and children love a special place to play. Children who have problems value somewhere safe to relax and cool down, they can hide in there or invite others.

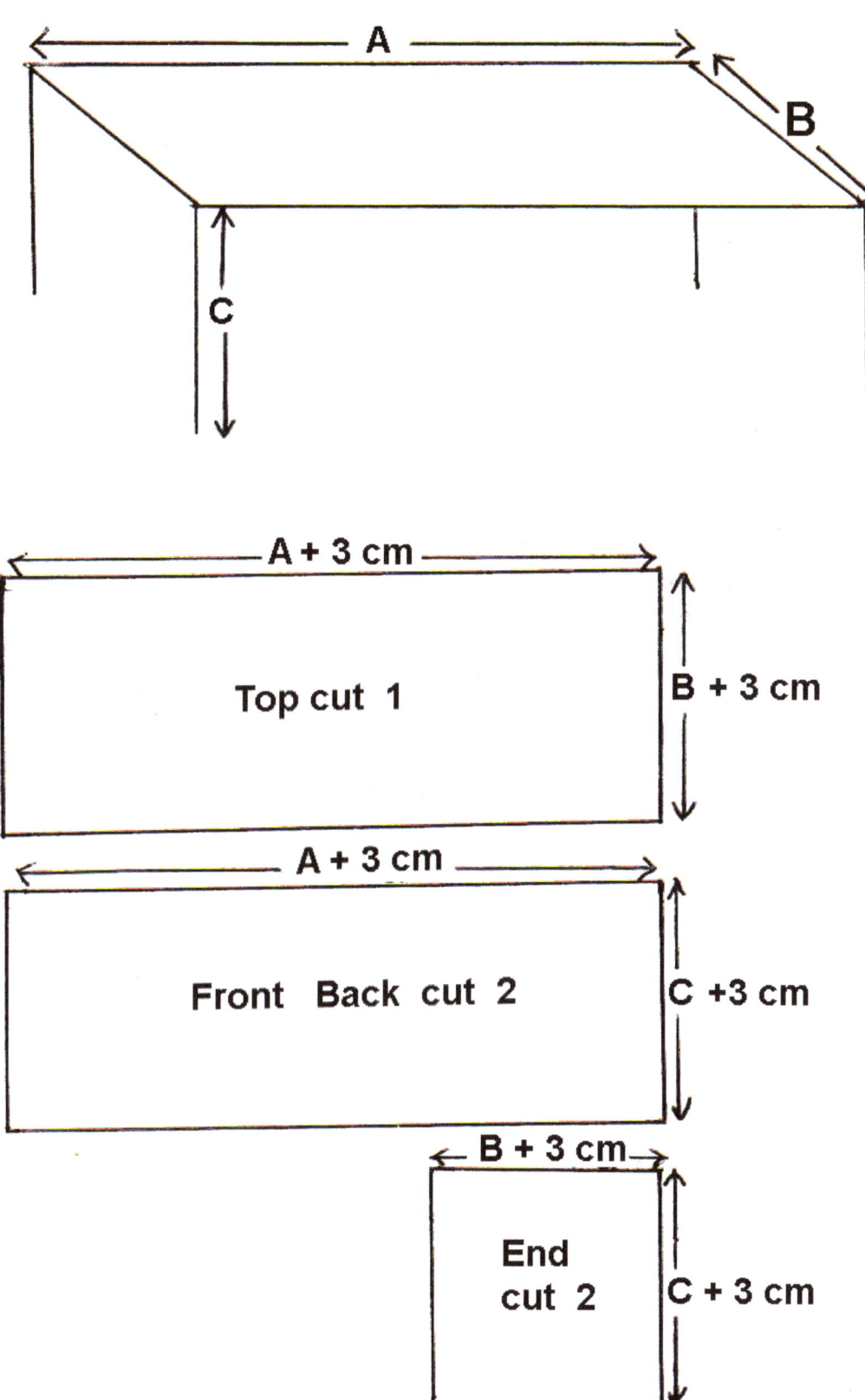

Materials:

1 queen sized sheet or curtains or

> new fabric 5 ½ m for 1mx1m table, 6 ½ m for 1m x1 ½ m table

Contrast if using 1.7m for small and 2.3m for longer table

Fly screen in plastic 2 pieces 30x36, one 26 x 18cm (30cm from 1m roll)

Cutting out:

If you are using a contrast for roof or windows do this first, then put the pieces aside still pinned to the pattern. This simple procedure saves getting the pieces mixed up or wrong way round.

Still using contrast for windows cut 2 pieces 30 x 36 and the same in mesh, 62cm x42cm in contrast and 26cm x 18cm mesh for door, this can be a different colour to the roof and or windows.

Now cut out the walls. That is two long sides and two shorter sides for rectangular tablecloth.

Method:

It is much easier to do the windows and doors before you assemble the whole cubby as you can lie them nicely flat to get clean edges.

Lay screen mesh on the back of the side pieces where you want the windows. Near the top but with at least 6 cm clearance, and fairly central works best. Pin at right angles to the edges of the mesh. Sew 1.5 cm from edges with thread matching the walls. Turn to the right side.

If you are not using contrast fabric, carefully lift the fabric from the mesh and cut in the centre of fabric, avoid clipping the mesh. Now that the scissors can safely cut the fabric, trim to 2cm from the stitching.

Cut diagonally towards the corners .5cm. Fold under a .5cm hem and stitch. This will give you a neatened 1.5cm frame round the window.

If you are using contrast fabric, cut two pieces of contrasting fabric, one for each window. Pin the contrast on the right side directly above the stitch line of the screen. Tuck under a narrow hem all round and stitch with thread matching the contrast fabric. If you have water erasable fabric pens fabulous! You can put marks everywhere to help you. If you do not have these pens use chalk or pencil and make sure the lines that you draw are on the folded under section.

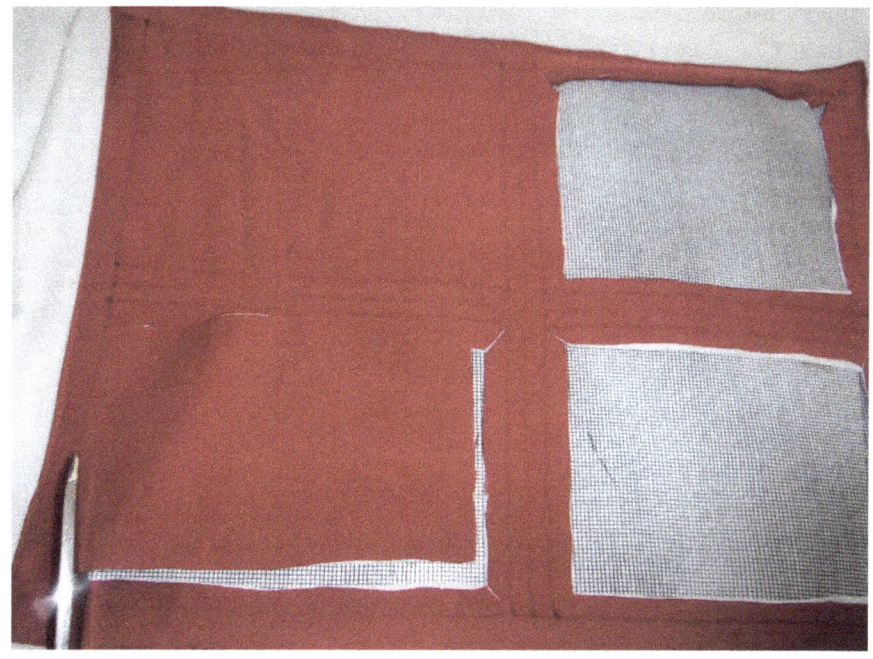

Window construction lines

Mark out the window frames showing fold lines. 1.5cm to 2cm looks best. Pinch up the fabric above the mesh and put a small nick to let the scissors in. Cut clear of the fold lines with a diagonal nick in the corner to the fold line. Pin down the centre of the frame in both directions. Now fold under hems and pin or tack in place. Sew as close to the edge of the hem as possible in the matching thread.

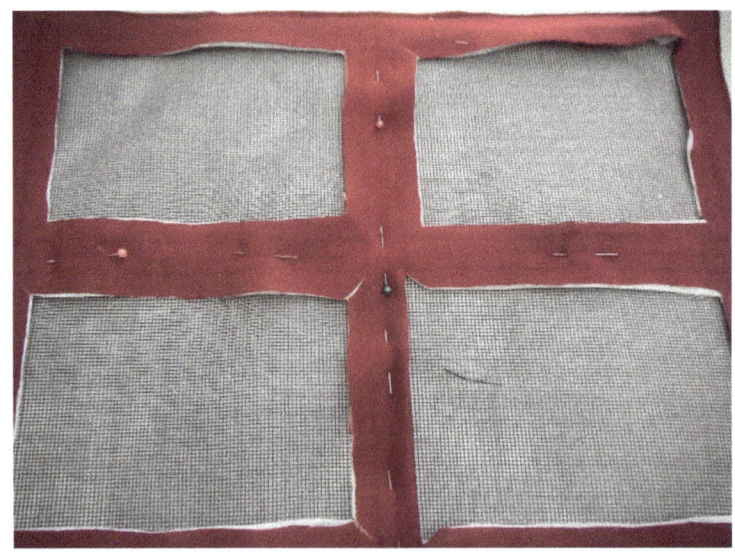

Partially pinned cut out window frames. Bottom right frame is partially folded ready to sew.

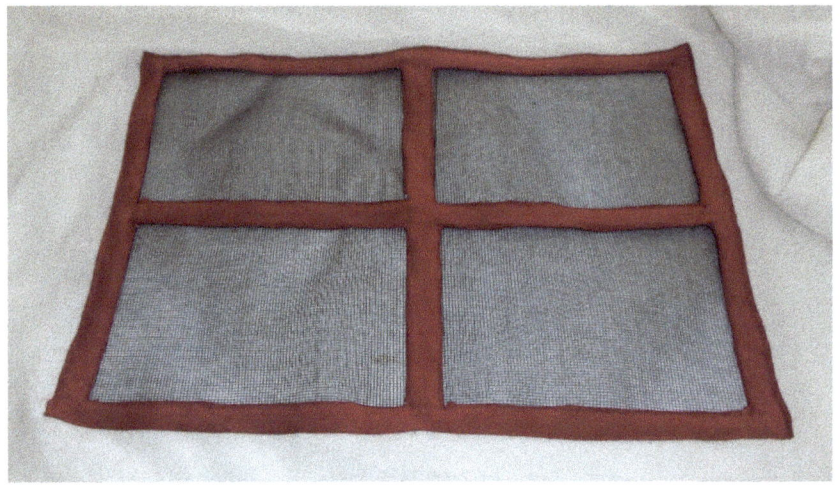

Stitched window frames.

Put the sides with windows complete to one side. Select one end to add the door.

If you are not using contrast either leave out the door or paint one on later. The windows will provide sufficient ventilation.

If you are using contrast cut a piece 62cm x 42cm (or the size of your offcut) and cut 26cm x 18cm in mesh.

Centre the door on the end panel with bottom of door with the hem turned up matching the bottom of the end piece. Pin the door tucking under 1.5cm seams all round and sew close to the edge. Carefully pin the screen on the back where you want the window feature (children like to look through the door to see who is visiting, but you can leave this out).

Follow the instructions for the window concerning pinning, cutting and stitching the frame.

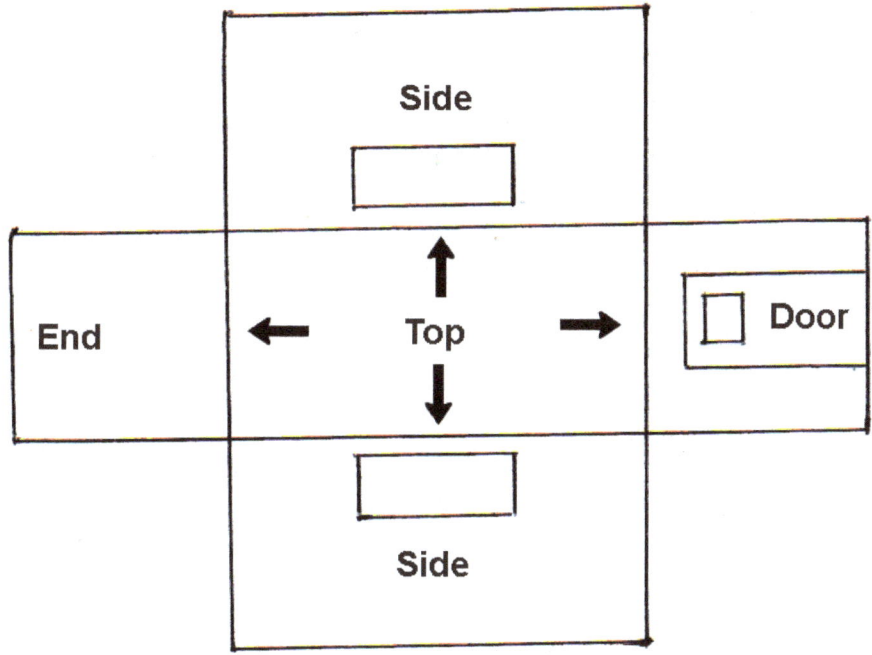

Placement of pieces to sew.

Using the diagram above as a guide, on the inside, pin the pieces together ready to sew. Make sure that you are working on the inside or this will end in tears.

Now for the easy bits. Pin the top of the ends to the shortest sides of the roof. Stitch a 1.5cm seam, *but do not stitch the first or last 1.5cm.*

Pin the sides to the top making sure the windows are closest to the roof. Sew 1.5cm seam, but do not stitch the first or last 1.5cm.

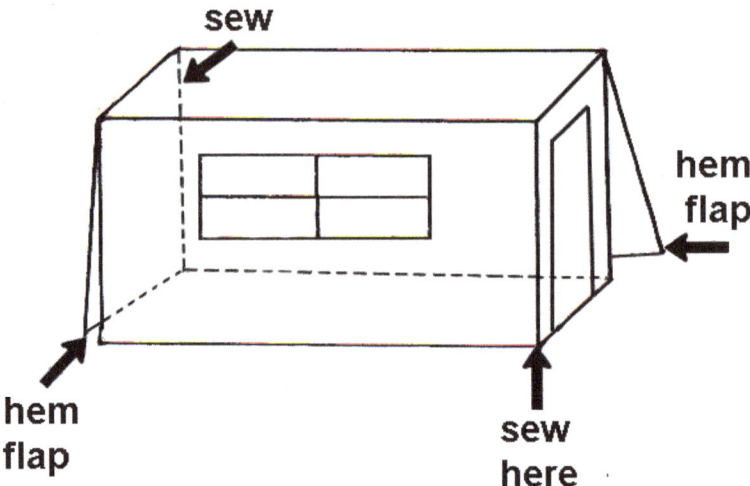

Sew front to one side, 1.5cm seam. Neaten this seam.

Sew back to the opposite side, 1.5cm seam. Neaten this seam.

Hem 1.5cm side front, side back seams. These are left open for the children to enter and leave.

Zig zag or overlock all-round the top. Hem any raw edges at the bottom that you have not already done.

Turn right side out.

Press if it needs it, but be careful with the fly screens.

All done!

A 1m square card table is a versatile addition to a small house or flat, it provides an extension to the dining/ kitchen table when visitors arrive, a picnic or craft table, and folds flat behind the curtains. I have used one of these for my demonstration model. If you are giving this as a gift and feeling generous, you may buy an inexpensive one to go with the cubby tent.

Using the methods shown in book 1 you can applique flowers around if you wish.

Cubby with flap door and roll up awnings

At a later date you may wish to get offcuts of lace curtaining to stitch inside the windows with ties to tie them back. You could also do shades on the outside (rectangles of fabric with ties either side to roll up). Variations are limitless. Remember everyone should be having fun here. You should have the sense of achievement having made it, and the children playing in it. It also makes a seriously fancy tablecloth. If sewing this becomes a drama, stop, try another day. If it still is a drama, give it to a friend who loves sewing with the instructions. All sewing disasters are dusters, recycle it.

Sew with joy and a sense of achievement or buy ready-made. Find your joy, do that and trade with someone who loves sewing if sewing is not your joy. You may find that your children are better at sewing, celebrate that. If you have learned something new or had fun, I have succeeded.

If you wish to share your efforts with me info.felixpublishing@gmail.com and I will reply. If you wish to make these projects to sell please contact us and gain permission first or you are breaching copyright, that is stealing by another name. We usually give permission for fundraising for charity.

Other books in this series **Make Life Simpler**

All are available as Kindle books or in printed form. This book is available as 6 individual booklets on Kindle as well as the full format.

The Perfect Assignment

Debt Free the Morals of Money Management

Libre de Deudas

Swift, Simple, Sweet…..

www.ingramcontent.com/pod-product-compliance
Lightning Source LLC
Chambersburg PA
CBHW041657040426
R18086800001B/R180868PG42333CBX00008B/7